YES, YOU CAN!

Yes, You Can!

AN INNOVATIVE APPROACH TO HAPPINESS

RAYMOND LEMKE

OMAHA PRESS PUBLISHING COMPANY, INC.
OMAHA, NEBRASKA

Published by Omaha Press Publishing Company

Reproduction or translation of any of this book, other than that permitted by Section 107 or 108 of the 1976 United States Copyright Act, without the express written consent of the author is prohibited and unlawful. Requests of permission or further information should be addressed to:
Consent Division
Omaha Press Publishing Company
8045 L. Street, Suite 1
Omaha, Nebraska 68127.

Library of Congress Cataloging-in-Publication Data
Lemke, Raymond L.
      Yes, You Can! An Innovative Approach to
      Happiness.
1. Happiness
I. Title
BJ1481.L46 1988 158'.1 88-61002
ISBN 0-9290-99-00-1

Printed in the United States of America.

About the Author

Raymond Lemke is a noted speaker on Personal Happiness and High Productivity.

He believes that life is not complicated—we only like to think it is so that we can justify our decisions and action.

He believes that each of us can have an immediate impact on our personal and professional lives by becoming more conscious of our own thoughts and environment.

He has written this book to show how easy it is to make the changes in YOUR life that YOU desire by utilizing YOUR natural abilities.

ACKNOWLEDGEMENTS

My very special thanks to Lucie Wilcox who has been very generous with her time and energy during the creation of this book. Her encouragement and support never waivered and were invaluable in bringing this book into existence.

My thanks to Bill and Nedra Conboy and George P. Miller for all their interest and support during the writing of this book. And for taking time from their busy lives to read the original draft and offer their suggestions and encouragement.

THIS BOOK IS DEDICATED
TO ALL THOSE WHO RECOGNIZE
AND SEEK OUT
THE HIDDEN OPPORTUNITIES
THAT ARE ALWAYS A PART OF
CHANGE.

--CONTENTS--

INTRODUCTION

PART ONE--Programming Change: Your Voice
Activated Personal Computer--

PART TWO

PART THREE--Re create Yourself!--

--The Quest for Personal Happiness--

I kept hoping I'd wake up and discover it was all just a bad dream. But the nightmare was real! My world was falling apart!

What had started out as a promising and exciting business venture was turning into a disaster. I had felt as though I was in on the ground floor of what I thought would be the Model-T of the airways in helping to create and distribute a small auto gyro two-place airplane that the average person could afford to fly out of his own backyard.

Then one of the trusted managing partners gathered up the available assets and left town. It left me and the other people involved totally crushed, mentally and financially. All of our dreams and efforts were invested in this venture.

As my thirty-fifth birthday neared, I became very depressed.

I realized my life was probably half over—at least according to the insurance tables. I began to wonder what my life was really all about. Was it ever going to get any better? Or was this all there was? I started to question my educational background, my abilities and talents, and even the very basis of my lifestyle—being married and having children. I asked myself, "Is this what life is all about?"

"Is this the way it's going to be the rest of my life?"

My future looked extremely bleak. I considered filing for bankruptcy. I even contemplated simply disappearing, running away from it all. By hard work and perseverance I had overcome several handicaps, but this was just too much. I just couldn't get up again!

Or could I?

I knew I was at a crossroad in my life, and I felt I had to decide what was really, truly important to me. If I was going to strive for something it ought to be the one thing that was far more important to me than anything else.

And, finally, after much thought, I decided that the most important thing to me was my personal happiness.

Now, at first, I'll admit that seemed like a selfish choice. But then I began to realize that the greatest gift I could give my wife was a very proud, happy husband. And the greatest gift I could give my children was a proud, happy parent. In fact, the greatest gift I could give to anyone was a very proud, happy Raymond! So, no longer believing it was selfish, I decided to devote the rest of my life to seeking out and perfecting personal happiness.

Then, as I became more AWARE of what really, truly made me happy, I noticed I was BECOMING happier. And as I became a happier person, I was also becoming a more productive person.

The pieces of the puzzle were starting to fall together. **The changes that were occurring in my life began to suggest to me that there might actually be some link between happiness and productivity.**

That realization was a major turning point in my life. The change that had seemed to be a terrible disaster only a few months before was actually the begining of a whole LIFETIME OF CHANGE that I've embraced and enjoyed. And that change has also brought me a great deal of professional success!

It was the beginning of a journey on which I've discovered that YES, YOU CAN really RECREATE YOURSELF for a lifetime of success and personal happiness.

This book, then, is my story. You'll find, however, that it's not an autobiography. Instead, it's a book about YOU. You see, I'm absolutely convinced that you share the same potential that I discovered in myself at age 35, and I'm very enthusiastic about awakening that potential in anyone who's willing to listen.

You can learn to control the natural connection between your thoughts and your actions. The process of positive personal transformation is available to you, beginning right NOW.

PART ONE

Programming Change:
Your Voice-Activated
Personal Computer

--Choose Change!--

How do you *really* feel about change?

We are challenged daily by change. Unfamiliar situations, different personalities, and unique problems confront us at every turn. Change is a critical factor for all of us, a puzzle we must constantly analyze and deal with. Whenever we face change, consciously or not, we make a choice. You can resist change, you can be passive towards it, or you can **CHOOSE** change.

As human beings, we are basically adaptable creatures. We're programmed in a special way to receive new information, process it, and act accordingly. Through our mental processes, we change ourselves in small ways to accommodate the changes we experience. We literally RE-CREATE ourselves in response to every change we encounter.

And we're so naturally skilled at coping with change that no matter what the challenge, we generally survive change. Occasionally we even master it. When things go well, we call it "luck." And we try to remember what wonderful combination of four-leaf clovers and correct behavior brought the matter to such a fortunate conclusion.

Still, when it comes to luck, we harbor a suspicion that there is some **trick** to it.   Some way of assuring that good rather than disaster will come out of change.   So, buoyed by this belief, sometimes we even initiate change.

We decide to work harder, move to a better apartment, overcome a bad habit, try a new hairstyle, or in some way become more the person we inwardly aspire to be. And whenever we choose change, we subconsciously expect to be rewarded for our efforts—with a promotion, compliments, new friends—some outward sign that proves that our efforts were worthwhile.

But perhaps because we spend so much time just reacting   to change, we're wary of taking on more unnecessarily.   So we approach our self improvement projects tentatively, calculating that we are being realistic in not expecting too much.   Too often we set goals which are too easily attained and then later are disappointed with what "life" has dealt us.

It's in these situations that our thoughts turn to that small group of people who seem to have been born under a lucky star—for whom everything they touch turns to gold. And half ashamed of our envy we wonder: what is the secret of their success?

And if we do venture out and fail, our self-esteem plummets and our productivity and happiness seem to fail along with it. We decide that it might be better to stay in the shelter of the status quo—with its security and comforts as well as its compromises.

When it seems that change may arbitrarily bring only either extremely limited success or dismal failure, who would go around looking   for change—actually seeking it out?

I WOULD! And hopefully so would you!

You see, I deliberately and successfully change

careers every ten years.

In fact, I do it with such consistency and regularity that by now my family and friends have learned to anticipate my career shift. "Well, what are you going to do next, Ray?" they begin to ask me as the sixth year of every decade approaches.

In my lifetime I've been a barber and a dance instructor. I've owned a large real estate company and a very successful insurance agency, and have had a private counseling practice—so far. Admittedly, some of my early career changes were more reactions than choices. For example, I knew I had to get out of the dancing business fast when I lost several toes in a lawnmower accident!

But then, at the time of that crisis in my life at age 35, this pattern of change became deliberate. I actively began to seek out and create enormous changes in the very nature of my daily activity and personal livelihood. Now I've embarked on another new career as a professional speaker. I view this as one more opportunity to increase my personal productiveness, happiness, and self esteem—the essential components of success.

How do you *really* feel about change?

Am I unusual? Perhaps! But why should the prospect of change be so frightening to us?

Before you write me off as an eccentric (or perhaps as one of those accidentally lucky types), stop to consider whether the process of personal transformation might not already be at work within you.

For example, do you ever talk to yourself?

Have you ever repeated a person's name when you're first introduced, as though saying it out loud will help you remember it? Or have you ever reminded yourself in an empty room, "I've got to call Mabel this afternoon?" Have you mentioned to your colleagues that you're "not very good at math"—and then proceeded to prove it each time you try to balance your checkbook?

Perhaps you've even tried rehearsing in the mirror, as you've shaved or combed your hair, for an important meeting later in the day. Of course, that's when you say all the right things—clever, witty, intelligent—for the occasion ahead.

And what about daydreaming? Do you ever do that?

Have you ever leaned back from your desk in a quiet moment at work, closed your eyes, and imagined yourself suddenly *transformed* into someone wealthier, more successful, more attractive, happier in your personal relationships, with a greater sense of self esteem—perhaps even to the point of being famous for possessing such an unusual combination of wonderful characteristics?

If you've ever done any of these, you already have some experience with the actual ingredients involved in personal happiness and high performance. You've flirted with success, danced once around the floor with it . . . and then perhaps stumbled over how to ask for another dance.

But success is **not** an accident. It's not some enchanted evening—to be savored once, and remembered nostalgically because it's unlikely to be repeated. **You can actually recreate yourself to be successful, and to enjoy the direct connection between productiveness and personal happiness.**

High self esteem is the link between accomplishment and personal happiness; it completes the circle that is success. When you profile the characteristics of people who feel good about themselves and are high producers, you will discover that people with high self esteem take greater risks and assert themselves more. Success produces high self esteem, and high self esteem enables the high achiever to extend himself, producing even more success.

These are the people who attempt the unthinkable—who accomplish the transformation most of us only dream about. **These are the people who have decided to take charge of change.**

High achievers do not believe that their success is mainly the result of any unusual talent or ability. In fact, they are frequently sincerely modest, and they consider themselves to be very "normal" people. Golfer Jack Nicklaus is said to attribute only 10% of his success to actual skill in hitting the ball. Sam Walton, founder of the extraordinarily successful Wal-Mart Stores, is indistinguishable in manner and appearance from all of the other residents of the small Arkansas town where he began his chain and continues to live today.

These people are not lying or being falsely modest. They consider themselves to be normal because they are normal, relying on the same basic trait that we all share—the conscious mind that distinguishes human beings from all lower life forms.

Happy, highly productive people are not born—they are made. Successful people have developed specific—but very natural—creative skills that reinforce their self-images and constantly open to them new vistas for productivity. High achievers know that the high self esteem they so depend on is not something you are born with, and not just something you end up with because you happened to have the right genes and caring teachers. Productive people understand that high **self esteem is nothing more than a way of taking responsibility for the way you talk to yourself and the way you** *visualize* **yourself.**

For example, if you've ever talked to yourself, you are familiar with the powerful effects of the well documented capacity of the human voice to affect mental processes and resultant behavior. It's the phenomenon of the *self-fulfilling prophecy*, and as you know, the results can be either positive or very negative.

When you decide to take charge of change, you begin to create wonderful, positive self-fulfilling prophecies about yourself.

This book presents no extraordinary methods. Instead, it draws on current research in fields as diverse as biology, linguistics, and the behavioral sciences, and the discussion and techniques described here are based only on what are absolutely normal attributes in all human beings.

Recent discoveries in these fields demonstrate that our definition of what is "normal" has been far too limited. Human beings really are psychologically and genetically designed to be healthy, happy, productive and successful. **Human beings have the potential to recreate themselves as they visualize themselves.**

Success is a journey rather than a destination, and change marks each step along the way. Because the human brain is a unique achievement, only human beings are capable of making the journey. Because you are human, because you can talk and think and visualize, you are poised now to embark on an incredible journey.

You may not be interested in changing careers entirely, as I have over the years. But you are probably interested in greater success and productivity in your present work. Certainly you seek to discover, as we all do, greater personal happiness and self esteem. To travel towards success and personal fulfillment is to embrace change and personal transformation—with the joy of challenge rather than a fear of failure, confident in the attributes and techniques already available within you.

Begin the journey now. You can add another major turning point in your life **TODAY**.

--Standing on the Turning Point--

Our culture has a deeply ingrained view that time is linear. We perceive life as a rather bumpy road along which we travel through the span of a lifetime. Change is seen as an abrupt turn along the way, into the unknown. Or we think of it as a fork in the road, where alternate paths demand hard choices on our part.

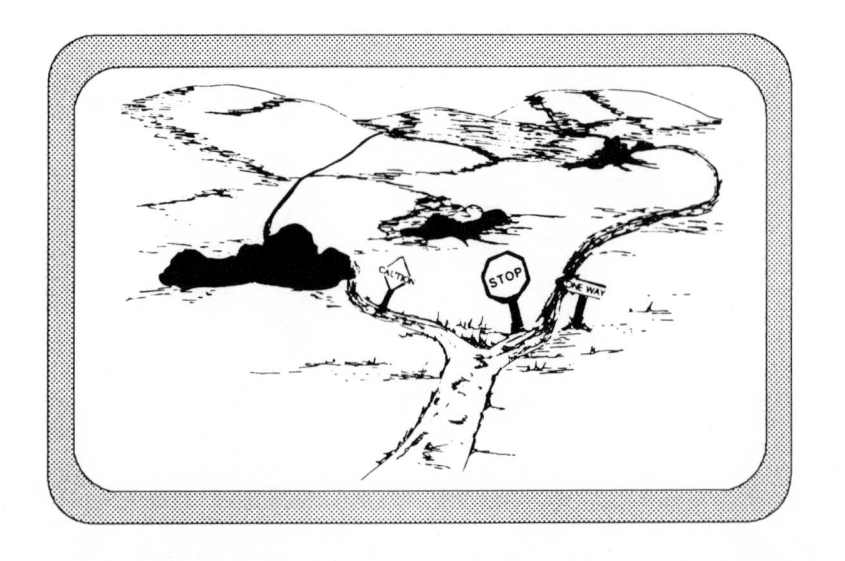

"Two roads diverged in a yellow wood . . . " wrote the poet Robert Frost in his famous and haunting, representation of this idea. We understand that these alternate routes—these choices—may lead to very different outcomes. And with many of the changes inevitabiy confronting us, we suspect that there is a "wrong way" and a "right way."

We're torn in our beliefs about how to choose the right path. We have a fairly strong belief in blind luck. Think, for example, of the enormous number of people who play state lottery games. On the other hand, our culture teaches us that hard work and intelligence will lead us to make good decisions when we face change.

But frequently there are no street signs along the journey, and "the untravelled road" is an ominous and compelling image in one's imagination.

Instead of envisioning ourselves as travelling down a road, we sometimes think of ourselves as adrift in a spinning universe where we come in contact with people and events in an apparently random fashion. We only sense an unexplainable energy in them. It seems that it is this energy—positive or negative—that forges change, as though by chemical reaction. As a result of this energy, we connect or spin off again, only to come in contact with other people and experiences, by chain reaction or powerful repulsion, throughout life.

While this might seem a more modern view of change, related to space travel and our growing scientific awareness of the shape of the universe, it is actually an even more ancient perception of reality. It remains the foundation for most Oriental philosophies today.

No one can say where the truth actually lies, but both views are useful. They provide us with a heightened, conscious awareness of who we are and why we behave as we do. If you are used to thinking one way, the other point of view can offer you a new perspective.

The first, a typically Western view, emphasizes goals and the way we approach them. This can-do, goal oriented approach has traditionally been one of the strengths of the European and American mentality. It produced the British and other European overseas empires, and it continued the westward expansion in America and created the industrial revolution.

But the second outlook highlights a fact that we Westerners tend to overlook or even dismiss—that there is an energy in this world that exists as both an influence on us and a resource for our individual use. The great emphasis on the natural world in oriental art, the profound mysticism of eastern religions, and the enormous success the Japanese have had in the cooperative approach to industrial and technological development are all manifestations of this life view. There is a strong suggestion that tapping into this energy, and achieving harmony with it, is indeed the source of happiness, productiveness, and the consequential fulfillment in life.

And, really—for those of us who have been trained to think of life as a linear journey—isn't this fulfillment exactly what we hope to find on our journey along our road in life?

Much of what you will learn from this book comes from some behavioral science research I've been very interested in over a long period of time. Basically, the research looked into an observable phenomenon—why some people are so much more productive than others.

Behavioral research is scientific, and as such it is quantifiable. You can measure productivity, and you can actually separate productive people from less productive individuals according to numbers and percentages. What researchers observed again and again, in studying productiveness, is the 80-20 rule—that **20% of the people do 80% of the work (accomplishments and results) and that 20% of the people have 80% of the money.**

I don't care what organization you belong to. I don't care what kind of work you do. You can go into a sales organization, a classroom, a large professional office, or a retail store. **20% of the people are going to produce 80% of the results.**

Furthermore, the same 80-20 ratio shows up when the distribution of wealth is analyzed. A relatively small 20% of people own or control a very large 80% of the available wealth in the world. Taken together, these productivity and financial statistics suggest to us some highly useful information.

As a psychotherapist with a private counseling practice, my particular interest in this research had to do with the connection between this 80-20 principle and people's happiness. In counseling work, we find that 20% of marriages are happy. There also seems to be a direct, observable correlation between happiness and productiveness. In sports we see that 20% of the players score an amazing 80% of the points. In every field we find that not only is that 20% more productive and successful than the other 80%, they also report greater personal happiness and greater self-satisfaction.

My conclusion is that successful people are the ones who are doing something they truly enjoy. This is my definition of success. When people enjoy their work so much that, while naturally they couldn't work for nothing, they almost would . . . *this is success!*

"At a certain point I could have stopped working so hard and lived quite well," says British actress Glenda Jackson, "yet I still work with the same intensity as I did when I began, perhaps more. It has to do with a duty to one's own potential, with unfolding and expressing one's capacities to the fullest."

In her study of high achievers, *Attaining Personal Greatness: One Book for Life* (William Morrow and Co., 1987), Dr. Melanie Brown concludes that happiness is the result of "purposeful action."

Successful people enjoy their work so much that they put more into it and derive more from it than other people do. Brown cites research that "shows that the vast majority of rich people became rich not because they were seeking wealth, but because they were profoundly absorbed in their work." The money just goes along with their overall fulfillmer t as an added satisfaction.

Itё lian painter Leonor Fini comments: "Work has always b⟩en the center of my existence: not work as somethinɡ one must do in order to earn money, but as an expressiori of creativity."

Thٍse people feel very good about themselves—because they are successful. They have high self esteern, and, of course, success validates high self esteem. Success says, "yes, you have a valid reason to think highly of yourself!" Success naturally reinforces one's belief in one's own worth and ability to be successful.

Remember that this group of people—the 20%—are

also successful because they feel good about themselves. **The natural by-product of high self esteem is a high degree of success.** This happiness-productiveness correlation appears to be a kind of circle, with happiness fueling productiveness and productiveness fueling happiness in an infinitely recycled pattern of perpetual continuity.

So high self esteem is essential to sustain peak performance and happiness. It's the link between these two components of success, and as such it's the logical point of entry into the happiness-productiveness cycle. **One needs to have high self esteem to become involved in the pattern of success.**

But where does high self esteem come from?

Aside from already having succeeded, how do we acquire it?

High self esteem is a way of being, rather than just positive thinking. **Self esteem is not simply an interior quality of the mind and thinking.** **It is also a way of engaging life, pursuing projects, and making plans. It is action as well as thought.**

We aren't used to thinking about self-esteem in this way. Our language doesn't even have a very good vocabulary for this concept. We don't say "he did a really good self-esteem today" or "she self-esteemed seventy-three times today."

But that's exactly how self esteem works. It is both thinking and the outward manifestation of thinking. In order to understand how concrete and vital self esteem is in our lives, we need first to examine the very real connection between our mental processes and our actual behavior.

--Everything In Life
Is Psychosomatic--

When I speak in public, near the outset of my speech I always ask the audience to relax and try to be as open as possible. I'm very aware that we all have a certain resistance to each other's voices. It's a very normal, natural thing, and probably impossible to fully overcome.

There is only one voice that you have no resistance to, and that's your own voice. So, as we shall see, its power is enormous and critical to your capacity to influence your own life.

The voices of others meet varying degrees of resistance from our mind. You can probably remember certain times when you were very relaxed and talking to a close friend. At these times, your friend could say almost anything to you, and your mind would not only accept it, but would accept it as fact. On the other hand, you might be talking to someone that you don't know as well. Then your mind resists the less familiar voice. Your mind is more hesistant to accept, and it filters the information more.

I encourage my audience to relax and be, quite

literally, *open-minded*, because I want to introduce to them a concept that might otherwise meet with considerable resistance. That idea is that **just about everything in this life is psychosomatic.**

A lot of people don't like that word—I suppose because they associate it with imaginary or fake illnesses. And while we're all convinced that our own ailments are extremely real, we tend to look down on people whom we think have dreamed up illnesses to get out of work or avoid dull social occasions.

But just about everything in life is psychosomatic. The term comes from the Greek, a combination of the words *psyche,* which means "soul" or "mind," and *soma,* meaning body. So the word literally means the interaction between the mind and the body, or physical reality. **To a very large extent, what actually happens to us is a direct result of what the mind believes—and the key word is "believes."**

Much of my research into this subject comes from the private counseling practice I maintained for a number of years. Psychotherapy is a perfect arena for this type of research. As a psychotherapist it was my role to ask questions, even though my inquiries might have nothing to do with why the person came to see me in the first place.

I found, too, that I usually got very honest answers to questions that really reached deep inside this other person's life. I soon realized that I was hearing many different versions of essentially the same story—over and over again! So the examples I use to illustrate my point, that everything in life is psychosomatic, are indeed true!

For example, there was the gentleman who said, "Every fall I catch a cold and then I've got a cold all winter long." You can just bet that in the fall he'll catch a cold and he's going to have that cold all winter long. You could keep him away from people who have colds, you could dress him properly, you could feed him the right foods, but it's not going to make one bit of difference. In the fall he's going to catch a cold and he's going to have a cold all winter long. It's psychosomatic, of course, but that doesn't make any difference. His nose runs and his throat is sore—it's a real cold! Because that's what his mind believes!

Fairly often in my practice, people would come in to see me because they were overweight. Since one-on-one therapy is rather expensive, generally by the time they came in to see me they'd already tried everything else. So they'd waste no time and would get right to the point. They'd say: "Now listen, I can go on a diet. I don't have any problems losing ten pounds, but I just gain it right back—plus a couple more pounds!"

And having heard that statement, there would be no doubt in my mind that these people would lose that weight—and that they were going to gain it back again, plus a little bit more. It's what their minds believed. **Self concept and performance go hand in hand.**

In my counseling practice, I also seemed to encounter a lot of people who would wake up in the middle of the night and then be unable to go back to sleep. And generally, in my experience, these were women (maybe the men just didn't want to admit this particular difficulty!)

A woman would come in to my office and say, "every morning I wake up at 2:15 and then I just can't go back to sleep and I'm tired all the next day." Since digital clocks have come out, it's even more specific: they've got it right down to the minute, 3:17 or 2:16. And sure enough, whatever the time, this woman is going to wake up right on the button. And she's not going to be able to go back to sleep, and she's going to be tired all the next day. Because that is what her mind believes.

Next, in doing this research, we tried something fun. In fact, you can do it right now—wherever you are. If you were to take a 20-foot four-by-four piece of lumber and lay it on the floor, you could see an impressive feat.

You could walk across that four-by four! In fact, you could walk across it without looking at it. One glance at it and your brain's got the picture. You could walk across the four-by-four, you could turn around on it, you could go backwards, sideways, and some people could even jump rope on it! You can do anything you want on that four-by-four because your mind knows you can do it. You wouldn't have any problems at all.

But, if I were to take that same 20-foot four-by-four and put it between two buildings with 35 feet of open air underneath it—and THEN asked you to walk across it, you'd freak out and you'd *refuse* to do it. But if you had to do it—if you were forced to—you'd get out there a few feet—*and you'd fall off.* There's no doubt about it. Because your mind would believe you were going to fall.

So you see, the mind can come to believe some fairly extraordinary things!

I was surprised, for example, to learn that in the metropolitan Omaha area where I work, there are some very sophisticated men who are scared to death of elevators. Now of course they know the elevator is safe. They understand the mechanics and the purpose of the elevator—many are even very mechanically inclined. But they also understand that if they get into that elevator, they are either going to scream, pass out, push the stop button, or do something else embarrassing and inappropriate. They don't want to behave this way, but because their minds believe they are going to, that is what will happen if they get into an elevator.

I found they are embarrassed enough to do all sorts of things to avoid elevators. Of course the first thing is they stay away from tall buildings. But when it's unavoidable, they go to great extremes to cover up their fear.

Let's say our friend and a colleague have to attend a meeting on the seventh floor of a building. He'll take charge immediately. He tells his colleague that he will pick him up at such and such a time, and they will go to the meeting together. But he'll be a little bit late and in a little bit of a rush. He'll walk in to the building with his colleague, he'll stride right up to the elevator—he'll push the button. Then just as the door opens, he'll say, "Oh, gee! I left my billfold in the car. I'll tell you what. You go on up and tell the others I'll be there in just a minute. I'm going to run out to the car and get my billfold."

He'll wait for the elevator door to close, and then like a shot he's up the stairs. And he's got the scenario all figured out about coming down, too, because he knows what will happen if he gets on the elevator. His mind knows exactly what he's going to do if he gets on that elevator. And yes, it will be embarrassing.

Just consider how much energy this man is expending on a belief he knows is absurd. **But this is the extent to which our minds control all of our behavior.**

Agoraphobics are another group. I was surprised to learn how many people there are in a city the size of Omaha who haven't been out of the house in ten or twelve years. They're just afraid to be out, anywhere, under any circumstances—even though they know their fear is unrealistic.

Actually, phobias are fairly easy to handle—people can get over them. But the point is that it's what the mind believes—it's psychosomatic. Phobics know their fears are ridiculous. They understand that perfectly well. But nevertheless their minds believe something else quite contradictory to what their good sense tells them. They feel completely divided. And it's no wonder!

Their feelings are completely natural. We all experience these conflicts because the human brain is by nature divided.

"We don't have a single united brain, but many small

brains with their own 'small minds'," write Robert Ornstein and David Sobel in *The Healing Brain* (Simon and Schuster, 1987). They explain that "this is one reason why we have such mixed feelings, mixed motives, and mixed messages, why we do things we don't wish to do, why we act sometimes almost out of our own control, why we are so susceptible to new and exciting events."

We need to remember that the brain is essentially an organ of the body. It is connected to the rest of the body neurologically and chemically, and its most important function by far is to regulate the rest of the body's functions-temperature, blood pressure, digestion, etc. Only a small part of the brain, the cerebral cortex, is the conscious mind involved in thinking, emotions and the other mental processes we usually associate with brain function.

However, the cortex is enormously important. Its development in man is what distinguishes human beings from other animals. In human beings only, it functions as a unique crossroad, where the external world meets our interior world. Through thought and language, the cortex is connected to the outside world of experience. Through emotion and imagination, it is connected to the internal operations of the rest of the body.

The cerebral cortex is itself divided in just this way. Language, mathematics, and other rational processes operate on the left side. But the right side of the brain is the site of creative, artistic, and most emotional life. Because it lacks language, the right side of the brain is silent and more mysterious. We generally understand the left side of our brains more easily because this part of our mental function is conversational.

The two sides of the conscious brain are not completely separate. They duplicate some operations, and they can communicate with each other. How the two sides are organized and how they transfer information to each other is not fully understoood—it is very complicated.

Scientists have examined a few very special individuals who lack the connection because it has been surgically severed to control very serious cases of epilepsy.

Julian Jaynes, author of *The Origin of Consciousness in the Breakdown of the Bicameral Mind* (Houghton Mifflin, 1976), states that these patients function surprisingly well in daily activity. But their unique deficits show how the connection between the two sides of the cortex would normally operate.

When scientists flashed random images in their right and left visual fields, an image of a nude woman flashed to the left visual field (received by the right side of the cortex) provoked grinning, blushing and giggling. Yet when the patient was asked the reason for the embarassment, the patient, using the left or speech hemisphere, replied that he had absolutely no idea.

In people with undamaged brain function, we can assume that communication between the two sides is lightning-quick and highly effective. Most people would be able to explain the source of their embarrassment in this situation! Images from the right side of the cortex can be explained verbally by the left side, and verbal input from the left side can create images in the right side. The left and right sides of the cerebral cortex usually work together.

Notice, too, that physical responses—grinning and blushing—are stimulated by the emotional right side regardless of the absence of input or understanding from the articulate left side. It seems that the right side is most closely tied to physical response.

So make no mistake about it. In the case of a power struggle between the two sides it is always the emotionally powerful right side that will triumph, no matter how many intelligent, logical arguments the intellectual left side of the brain presents to the contrary. The rational, logical part of the brain is quite powerless when the emotional, irrational part of the brain has accepted a compelling belief. Ask any phobic!

By now you may be beginning to wonder where I'm going with all this. Well, all of the anatomy, and all of the examples cited, are the foundation for the important information that will equip you to recreate yourself.

--Your *Voice Activated* Personal Computer--

In a discussion like this one, or in anything else in life, it's important to have a good foundation. When you build a house or start to make improvements, the first thing you must do is look at the foundation. **I believe that if you have a good foundation in life, something to really grow from and build on, it makes life a great deal easier.**

Taken together, the information and examples I've described in the previous chapter illustrate the power the psychosomatic connection has in our lives. Understanding the psychosomatic connection is the foundation for learning to take charge of this connection and use it for personal growth.

Although the problems I've described may not be exactly the ones you wrestle with in your life, you can probably identify with the basic dilemma. We have all had the experience of recognizing something we should or should not do while yet feeling powerless to act accordingly. We've all had that feeling of engaging in a long, chatty coversation with ourselves over conflicting impulses, one logical and the other purely emotional.

All of the individuals I've described seem to have a little defect in the foundations of their character. Something that prevents them from growing in the direction they'd like to. Something that makes their lives a little more difficult than seems really necessary. It's as though what their brains believe—emotionally, on that powerful right side—includes a little piece of wrong information in their program or blueprint that keep interfering with the building they're trying to accomplish.

The human mind, in all its complexity, is actually a wonderful, exceedingly sophisticated computer. It's such a fantastic computer that it makes the most advanced computer we have today look like a horse and buggy. But although our mind's computer is incredibly complex, it's very easy to program, because our personal computer is voice-activated. So, if you've spoken out loud to yourself as a memory aid, you have stumbled across the key to programming your own mind—programming it to remember a simple thing, such as the name of your new acquaintance, the address you're driving to, or the telephone number you must dial.

And if you've fallen into one of those negative self-fulfilling prophecies, you've encountered the same principle at work. Everything in life is psychosomatic—from that announcement that you're no good at math, to your friendly reminder to yourself to phone Mabel, to remarkable plans for future success. Good or bad, odds are that if you say it and believe it will happen . . . it's going to happen!

And you've ever daydreamed, you've tried creative visualization—another technique that high achievers use to maximize their potential. You've tapped into one of the essential interior mechanisms of the human mind. Visualization is simply using your mental eye like a movie screen inside the theater of your mind. Whatever you vividly and consistently imagine, you can bring to pass—within reason. The wonderful person you imagine yourself to be is an attainable goal because what your mind can conceive and believe—you can DO!

These two processes—verbal input and visualization—are the common, ordinary components of all positive and negative thought. Everyone thinks this way, because this is the way the human mind is constructed. In some people the process reinforces negative beliefs and supports negative outcomes. In others, the process is under utilized. Successful people have simply learned to use verbal input and visualization as complementary processes to maximize the great potential of this normal, human mental system.

You can take charge of change by understanding that the human mind is a voice-activated computer that interactively uses verbal input and visualization to cause ALL of your actions. **The mind both causes and responds to actual events in your real world.**

Its complexity and its divisiveness might lead us to believe that it's difficult or impossible to program the human mind. But in fact exactly the opposite is true. **If people only understood how easy it is for us to program our own minds, our accomplishments would be immeasurable. We CAN actually recreate ourselves.**

Each of us has a mind that is a voice-activated personal computer. And the voice to which it responds most strongly is our own.

Are you aware that when you say something out loud, the message comes out of your mouth and right back into your own ears? **And the message you say out loud has five to seven times more imprint capacity on your mind—more strength and more impact—than a mere thought.**

You understand this principle on a subconscious level whether you know it consciously or not. If you want to remember a name, you'll say it out loud. If you want to remember an address or a telephone number, you'll say it out loud. You're already familiar with this principle, and to some extent you probably employ it in your daily life.

If you were suddenly frightened and found yourself in a threatening situation, you would automatically start talking to yourself out loud. It's a natural phenomenon. You'd start giving yourself verbal instructions. And then you'd go back to logical thinking again.

Here's another example. Maybe this has happened to you. Let's say that you and five or six friends are at lunch, and you're very relaxed. Again, "relaxed" is a key word: *it means that your mental computer is receptive.* You've been looking at the menu and you're planning on ordering a bowl of soup. But perhaps the waitress takes several orders before yours, and someone orders a bowl of soup and a salad. Look out! There's a very strong possibility that you're going to order soup and a salad, too. **Because a message through the ear, even in someone else's voice, is far stronger than a message inside your own mind.** The mind, your mental computer, is designed to respond to suggestions in the external world.

You've probably had the experience of talking to someone who keeps repeating an explanation or a justification over and over again. Finally it dawns on you that he's not actually talking to you. He's still selling himself on whether or not he should have bought that new car or those new drapes.

We can talk ourselves into and out of anything by what we say out loud and what we allow other people to say out loud to us.

Now we can really begin to understand why that gentleman we talked about earlier catches a cold in the fall and has a cold all winter. Just listen for a little while!

One thing we've really learned to do in private counseling work is not to ask why. In answering, the person will validate the particular belief, it'll get back in his mind, and then the belief will be that much stronger. As the person speaks his answer out loud, he is reinforcing what he has already programmed his mind to believe—in this case, that he will catch a cold in the fall and have it all winter. Just become conscious of really listening!

We all see this process in action. I've had it happen to me on the phone. (And really, the phone is the best place for this type of conversation. If it has to happen at all—I prefer to keep my distance.) Someone will call me up on Monday morning and say, "Oh, do I have a terrible head cold! I'm so plugged up I can't hardly talk. I just know tomorrow it's gonna be down in my throat and by Wednesday it'll be in my chest, and by Thursday I'm gonna ache all over, and I just know I'm gonna have to take Friday off." Once you hear this litany, you might as well cancel any plans you have for him on Friday. He's going to be home sick. **Because that's what his mind believes!**

Why does that person lose that weight and gain it back? My goodness, *just listen!* The person will say, "oh, I can go on a diet. I'm on a diet right now, but in about ten days—I don't know. . . I just go *crazy* and I just eat everything that's in the house." And sure enough, it's about ten days on the nose, and that's the way it will happen.

Why does that lady wake up at 2:15 in the morning, can't get back to sleep? I don't know. It really doesn't matter. Maybe she had an upset stomach. Maybe she had to go to the bathroom. Maybe the dog barked. I don't ask.

But she gets up the next morning and is talking to her husband, saying something like "Oh, gee. I woke up again last night at 2:15 and I just couldn't go back to sleep. I rolled and tossed all night. I just know I'm gonna be tired all day long." And then she tells all her friends the same thing, she tells all of her aunts and uncles, she tells everyone that she wakes up, and now she's telling me that she wakes up at 2:15 and can't go back to sleep.

She doesn't need to tell me. I know that's going to happen because **that's what her mind believes.**

Smokers are a great example. Now everybody knows you shouldn't smoke. It's hard on your upper respiratory system and causes sinus drainage, it takes away from 18% to 22% of your energy—nobody wants to smoke! But you meet that smoker, and he'll say, "Oh, I know I shouldn't smoke. I've tried to quit and every time I've tried to quit, my left leg gets shorter than my right leg and I start to limp." Just let that person quit, and I'm not kidding you, you're going to see him start to limp—which justifies picking up a cigarette again. After all, he's got to cure that limp!

So understand how you limit your performance. **You are responsible for your responses and results, because there is a close, inextricable, psychosomatic connection between your beliefs and the concrete, actual results of those beliefs.** And it's this connection that lies behind the self-fulfilling prophecies we so frequently observe in others and experience in our own lives.

Have you ever heard someone make statements like these?

—I just can't seem to get caught up.
—I'm too old to learn new things.
—I just can't think until I've had my first cup of coffee.
—I already know I won't like it.
—I never have enough time.
—I can't make ends meet.
—I never get a break.
—I'm not going anywhere at work.
—No one appreciates me.

And then they think life is unfair when that is what they get. **Remember, life is a self-fulfilling** *prophecy!*

This connection is nowhere as evident as in matters of the physical self and health. For the brain is the organ that regulates all other bodily functions. Ornstein and Sobel, authors of *The Healing Brain*, have described an experiment in which blood pressures were monitored of people engaged in ordinary conversation.

Blood pressures rose as the individuals spoke and went down as they listened. Some individuals showed particularly high readings when they spoke of particularly emotionally charged subjects. The experimenters compared this response to "inward blushing," and they speculated that changing communication patterns might contribute to controlling blood pressure problems.

We can see that the brain's beliefs can cause actual, dramatic, physical responses. Here again, self esteem is the link. A person with high self esteem will not speak of his or her goals and efforts in negative, self-deprecating terms. But an individual with low self esteem validates negative beliefs by predicting negative outcomes. The psychosomatic connection guarantees that the outcome will in fact be as negative as predicted.

Become conscious of who you are and understand the programmed results of low self-esteem.

--Programming the Positive--

We've looked at a number of negative examples—instances in which people have programmed their mind with beliefs in negative outcomes.

But the mind also works in a positive mode.

Henry Beecher, who was chief of anesthesia at Massachusetts General Hospital and a professor at Harvard Medical School for many years, was a lifelong student of pain. In examining medical records of soldiers injured in battle in World War II, he noticed that the injured men's need for pain medication did not correspond to the severity of their wounds. In fact, it was the least badly wounded who required the most pain medication.

Beecher's research also led him to study the **placebo effect**. This well-known phenomenon occurs again and again in double-blind tests of new drugs, and researchers have learned from experience to always use adequate controls for such experiments. The power of suggestion and people's beliefs about the effectiveness of medication is such that people experience relief from symptoms when given a pill—even if the pill contains absolutely no active ingredients!

The placebo effect is even more powerful if the placebo pill is administered along with powerful verbal suggestion. When a doctor administers any medication, real or otherwise, with a strong suggestion that it is highly effective in treating the complaint, the medication is far more likely to be effective.

The mind's influence on human behavior extends far beyond purely medical phenomenons. For example, have you ever noticed that whenever you've become good at something—anything—in your life, it's at exactly the same time as when you first realize "hey, I'm pretty good at this!" Actually becoming accomplished is directly correlated with your recognition of your accomplishment.

Perhaps at this point you're thinking that yes, you understand the direction of this discussion. Perhaps you can even accept the line of thinking we've pursued so far, especially the idea that negative attitudes programmed into the brain can be damaging enough to actually cause a great deal of self-defeating behavior. But you may be reluctant to accept the other side of the coin of this argument—that positive beliefs can actually cause us to achieve our goals. After all, even if this were true, no one can be expected to go through life being positive all the time, can they?

YES!   It is possible!

"But," you might be thinking, "Everyone has a bad day once in a while, don't they?" No! That doesn't have to be true! In fact, that's like saying if you drive a car you have to have an accident every 25,000 miles. And that's certainly not true either!

Just as you must learn to be aware of bad driving habits you must learn to be aware of negative thoughts and attitudes.

You can learn to program your mind for positive outcomes and actual sought-after achievements. The placebo effect has far-reaching ramifications in all areas of our lives.

You learn to program the mind in exactly the same way you learn any skill—skiing, for example. When you begin to learn to ski, you fall down a lot. But soon, if you keep at it, you begin to make corrections. Then, as you start getting good at it, you constantly make minute corrections while you're going down the slopes. Whether you speak them out loud or merely think them as thoughts, those corrections are bits of information you're feeding to your mind, your own voice-activated computer. In turn, that computer is the mechanism that operates your body physically as you ski.

And does that computer ever work! It accomplishes great things—from coordinating your arms, legs, shoulders, eyes, and ears in a complex physical operation like skiing, to processing thoughts into concrete manifestations like scientific discoveries and great works of art.

At this very moment, millions of children are learning to walk and talk through precisely this method. They try a step and fall down, or they make a stab at a word and are met with blank stares. They have almost no experience, yet their mental computers make corrections very expertly, and the next thing you know, you have a couple of proud parents thinking they've taught the kid something!

Notice, too, that an instance of failure has nothing to do with the computer's ultimate success in mastering the operation. **In fact, failure is perfectly all right, in the sense that the corrections necessary to achieve the success arise out of initial failure.** In the skier's case, the initial attempt results in falling down. In recognizing how falling down happens, the mind's computer develops the corrections necessary to avoid falling down in the future.

Scientists operate by trial and error. They know that their solutions are not fully reliable unless other possibilities have been definitively rejected through experimentation. Sculptors make numerous sketches and clay models before taking chisel to marble. They eliminate inadequate designs before attempting a final, "perfect" version.

What does it take to weather the necessary errors that are frequently the prelude to achievement?

Again, the key is self esteem. Your self esteem should not be changed or diminished by failure if you understand that "failure" is often merely a course-correction along the journey to success. It is an opportunity for greater awareness. And awareness produces personal power and higher self esteem, as the recreation process continues.

Nor should rejection by others damage your self esteem. We have all heard stories of inventors whose efforts were ridiculed by the public for years while they worked to perfect their visionary creations. And of enormously gifted writers who survived years of rejection slips before their works were finally published. The astronomer Galileo was condemned and excommunicated by his church for describing the configuration of the solar system in a way that we know today to be absolutely correct.

You cannot prove your worth to others. It is both an interior and a subjective quality. You cannot definitively demonstrate it to others, nor should you try. Someone will always disagree. But you can realistically know your worth, for it is a matter of self esteem.

Self esteem is a personal characteristic. It is not dependent on the views or values of others. Not only is it okay to like yourself, it is okay to like yourself more. In fact you can't really like another person until you first learn to like yourself. Higher self esteem is always available.

--Your Mental Pictures—
Positive or Negative?--

Semantics, a highly specialized field, is the scientific and philosophical study of meaning in communication. It looks into how meaning is actually conveyed and understood in every imaginable kind of communication process. Linguists, anthropologists, and biologists share an interest in semantics. The use of language is, of course, one of the most important distinctions between human beings and lower animals.

The most basic principle of semantics was proposed in 1923 by C.K. Ogden and I.A. Richards in *The Meaning of Meaning*. They said that meaning actually has three components: an actual object, a person having thoughts about that object (in pictures), and a sign or symbol for it. Meaning does not exist unless all three components exist.

Let's take the very simple example Ogden and Richards suggested. If I wish to convey the idea of a "chair" to you, I first form a mental picture of a chair. This mental picture refers to an actuality: there really are chairs! Then I convey my mental picture to you by using an agreed-upon symbol, the English word "chair."

Your understanding of my meaning involves exactly

the reverse process: hearing the word "chair," you form a mental picture of a chair, and therefore understand the same actuality from which I started.

Communication can break down when we don't agree on the word or symbol for chair, as, for example, when I speak English and you speak French or Swahili. In the case of concepts more complex than "chair," communication can also break down if our mental images are too different. When the concept is "chair," it doesn't matter if I think of a straight-backed kitchen chair and you think of a purple, upholstered chair: we're close enough. But if we get into a different kind of actuality, like "liberty" or "propaganda," we could get into a great deal of difficulty if our mental images are significantly different.

Well, you can see why communication theorists are interested in this idea. My interest in the semantic theory is the important insight it offers us into the basic process of the human mind, our voice-activated computer.

The theory of semantics shows us that there is a very basic, highly significant connection between actuality, words, and mental images. Since Ogden and Richards' work, biologists and medical scientists have discovered a great deal about the structure of the human brain, so today an important correspondent is evident. The three elements of meaning correspond to the two sides of the cerebral cortex in the human brain and the external world they are designed to respond to. **When language activates our mental computer, it is activating mental images.**

Language is truly one of the keys to understanding the human mental process. And the improved use of communication is one of the keys to developing personal potential and the potential of our society. "Language is largely definitive of the human condition, essential for human thought, for human communication, for human learning, and for the new form of inheritance and of evolution that has arisen in man," says George Gaylord Simpson in *Biology and Man* (Harcourt, Brace, Jovanovich, 1969).

Alfred Korzybski, the founder of a special school of semantic thought called *general semantics,* believed that a great deal of commonly used language is vague and superstition laden. He advocated a radical revision of linguistic habits in light of the findings of modern science. Korzybski believed that changing the way we talk about things can change both our beliefs and our behavior.

And yet, as important as language is, we really cannot think except in pictures. Images run **constantly through our minds on a continuous tape, like ever-changing graphics on a computer screen, or a movie camera constantly panning inside the mind.**

This is our essential mental process; words are only an outward manifestation of the process or the trigger that prompts the process to begin.   Together, in the mind, pictures and words come together to produce a constant, documentary-style motion picture that is the mirror image of external reality.   And this is thinking, in its natural form, as all human beings experience it.

For an example, let's return to the skier we discussed in the last section of this book. He's just fallen down on the first run he's attempted, and the image he has in his mind is that of himself coming stiffly down the hill and collapsing awkwardly and painfully. He translates the mental picture into words:

"What did I do wrong?"

His ski instructor, having just witnessed the fall, has an equally clear picture in his mind.   But because the ski instructor knows how to come down the hill correctly, **his mind replaces the picture of the novice falling with an image of a skier coming down the hill correctly.**   So he says,

"Try bending your knees a little more."

His words produce a new image in his student's

mind, prompting the correction process we discussed previously. Actual better skiing is the result of their exchange.

Pictures in our mind always actualize our lives . These mental images prompt not only what we say but also what we do. The reason why you can walk across a four by four board on the floor but cannot go across it when it is suspended between two buildings is simply that you have such a powerful, compelling image of yourself falling from that height. Not only do you say, "I can't do that—I'll fall," you will in fact fall if you attempt it. It is not either a matter of luck or skill; it is simply a matter of the mental picture you carry.

Let's try a little mental experiment to understand exactly how mental images affect physical responses.

Imagine a lemon. It's a very yellow lemon, just a tiny bit green. Hold the lemon in your hand and smell it. You can tell it's very fresh and probably quite sour. Now take that lemon, put it on a cutting board, and mentally take a knife and cut it exactly in two. Notice its freshly cut, juicy surface. It's very cool and succulent.

Now pick up half of that lemon, open your mouth wide and bite down—right now! Taste its sour flavor.

You'll find that, involuntarily, your mouth puckers slightly and begins to salivate, just as it would if you were actually to bite into a lemon. Although the intellectual left side of your mind knows that there is no lemon, the picture in the right side of your mind is powerful enough to override the left side's objections and cause an actual, physical reaction.

Although the rational left side of your mind can intellectualize the difference between real and imaginary sourness, the right side of the mind is not able to discriminate between the two—nor does it even attempt to. **All images are equally real to the right side of the mind, and it is these mental pictures that ultimately govern our physical responses and**

behavior.

Remember that the right and left sides of the mind communicate very effectively. Remember, too, that both words and images are components of meaning and understanding. In the lemon example, words received by the left side of the brain triggered the image in the right side of the brain that produced the physical reaction in spite of the left side's rational objections. Both the left, language-oriented side of the brain and the right, image-producing side of the brain are involved in the complex mental process that creates actual, physical reality.

You can recreate your own life by understanding that mental pictures govern our actions, and you can take charge of the actuality of your life through the images in your mind. If you decide to take total responsibility, improve your self concept, and drop whatever has been unpleasant in the past, you will immediately produce an improvement in your performance and personal happiness.

Understand that if you play a very critical role with your self concepts, they will become you. And this is true in the positive sense just as much as it is in the negative.

The pictures in our minds always actualize our lives... always!

...whether negative...

CHILDHOOD AGONY
PAST FAILURES
UGLY

TOMORROW'S DREAMS
ACHIEVEMENT
BEAUTY

...or positive!

--The Garbage In/Garbage Out Rule--

In all cases of achievement, from the great artist or scientist down to the ordinary child taking his first steps, we see a process by which information programmed into the mental computer can set positive goals and provide meaningful corrections. But we've looked at plenty of examples of negative programming, too—instances in which people who believe themselves unworthy create proof to support that belief.

Why is high self esteem so difficult to achieve and sustain?

Self esteem is fragile and vulnerable to the criticism of others because, like a computer, the mind doesn't judge initially. It accepts everything it hears. Although, as we've noted, the mind is most receptive to the sound of one's own voice, there is no absolutely filter on that voice activated computer. I can lead you in quite an unexpected direction simply by writing a few words about lemons. The spoken word is even more compelling. This is the reason why parents are rightly concerned about their children's companions. Whatever is said to those children inevitably will have an effect of one kind or another on them.

Some important research on this subject stemmed

from a 1973 bank robbery in Sweden that ultimately gave its name to the effect—**the Stockholm Syndrome.** After the hostages in the Stockholm case were held for a while, they began to see their captors as heroic, and later they even refused to testify against them.

If someone is kidnapped and held under extremely desperate circumstances, before long the victim will begin to think and act like the kidnappers. You will recall that in this country, Patty Hearst's main legal defense after her 1974 abduction and long ordeal was based on this acknowledged phenomenon. Her attorney, F. Lee Bailey, argued that mental strain caused her to identify with her Symbionese Liberation Army captors and their violent revolutionary ideals. More recently, a similar pattern has been observed among some hostages held in Iran and other parts of the Middle East.

Despite our natural resistance to another's voice, clearly the brain's capacity to accept negative input from others is still very great. I know that this is an extremely strong statement, but I'm as serious as I can be when I say that **I'm more afraid of a negative person than I am of cancer.**

I'm scared to death of a negative person because I know that if I let that negative data into my mind, it's going to start to work influencing me. It happens easily. I'm sure many of you have had the experience of going to work bright-eyed and bushy-tailed, feeling great, only to encounter one of the doom-and-gloom-sayers. The first thing you know, you're feeling all down too.

I'm not the first person ever to observe this cause-and-effect relationship, either. Long ago an anonymous preacher commented in Proverbs 22:24-25:

> *Don't make friends with people who have*
> *hot, violent tempers.*
> *You might learn their habits and not be able*
> *to change.* (Good News Bible)

Be extremely conscious of everything that goes into your voice-activated computer!

You must at all times be extremely conscious of the input into your mind. If you actually had a voice-activated computer sitting on your desk at work, all wired up and plugged in to pick up everything that was said so that it would have an effect on you, you'd be extremely conscious of what you would allow others to say in your office.

Well, you do have a voice-activated computer, right between your ears, and there's no filter on it. It not only sits at your desk, it also goes everywhere with you.

People who work with computers have a saying: "garbage in, garbage out." They mean that you can't expect your computer to do a good job if you program it poorly or enter poor data.   It's your obligation to protect your computer from negative data. People cannot put you down, nor can they put down your values or your worth or your accomplishments, unless you allow them to do so.

The influences that affect you can be a little like the alchoholic in the latter stages of the DT's who comes in to see the doctor. "Oh, Doc, help me," he says, brushing his hands wildly all over his clothes. "I've got these snakes crawling all over me!" But the doctor tells him, "You son of a gun, don't you dare brush them off onto me!"

That's the way I feel about negative people: I don't want them dumping their negativeness on me!

How do I go through life being positive all the time?

Take watching the news, for example. Of course you will hear some negative things if you watch the news with any regularity. But when I see something I don't agree with, I imagine that I'm in a decision making position for that particular situation. I ask myself what I would do under those circumstances and **I go for the positive solution.**

If it's raining out, a negative person would be apt to walk in and say to me, "Oh, what a lousy day." Be extremely conscious of what another person is selling. Where this self-appointed weatherman is going is not exactly clear, but with an opener like that, you can be sure that what he has to sell is negative.

It's *my* computer, and I know this remark is going to have an effect on me. So my reaction is to cover it up right away. If I don't get the negative input covered right away, I know it's going to go into my computer and though pattern. So I say something, almost anything, to override the negative idea. "Yeah, but the rain is good for the subsoil moisture, and it's great for the grass." You must say something positive. *And remember, your own voice has a more powerful influence than another person's voice. Your positive statement will override the negative statement in your mind.*

I'll never forget a particular November morning. The weather had turned quite cold very suddenly. I had a long drive to make that morning and had stopped at my office to pick up some files before leaving town. It was extremely early in the morning when I arrived—a time when normally there would be no one in the building.

I was in the rest room washing my hands when another man walked in and started saying the most terrible, nasty things about the weather. In fact, the language he was using to describe the weather shouldn't be used even in the men's rest room!

My day had hardly begun and already I was hearing this barrage of negative comments! I knew I had to counteract this incredibly accidental, negative start to my day with something positive, and, as I've said, almost anything will do. So I said to this stranger who was dumping his negativeness on me, "Yeah, I was out there. But one thing I also noticed was that there weren't any mosquitoes out there." And I hurried, dried my hands and left as quickly as possible.

I suppose these weather-related examples come to mind because, despite technology's success in circumventing natural conditions, we are still profoundly affected by the natural world. We have a tendency to become gloomy on a rainy day, and some people are miserable when they have to work inside on a glorious one. People talk about the weather all the time, and it's incredible that, more often than not, they have something negative to say about it.

Learn instead to be sensitive to the natural world in a positive way. See it as an occasion for a reversal of the negative you will surely hear and as an opportunity for innovation.

Your own voice has a more powerful influence than another person's: your positive statement will override the negative in your mind!

So you planned to go boating and now it's raining? Find a creative alternative. Analyze your roof and gutters for that leak you have been meaning to fix. Read something useful or purely enjoyable. Spend time with family or friends. Write or telephone those who need most to hear your message of affirmation.

Feeling frustrated because you are cooped up inside on a beautiful day? Make plans to at least eat your lunch outside—or skip it entirely, if that's what's good for you—and go for a walk instead. Be the schoolteacher who throws the lesson plan to the wind and takes the class outside for an experiential lesson. If some flexibility is available to you, make a project of finishing your work early. Be willing to set goals and reorder your priorities quickly. **Be extremely conscious and seize the opportunity now.**

So, you see, you can do it! You **can** override the negative with something positive. In fact, it's your obligation to do it, because it's your computer. It's your responsibility to see that positive input enters your computer so that positive results will come out of it. And nowhere is this more important than in what you allow to be spoken aloud to you.

I'm constantly amazed when I talk with people. They always want to tell me everything about their bad knee; they never want to tell me about their good knee. They want to tell me about everything that went wrong that weekend instead of about all the good things that happened. I'm amazed that some people seem to find so much identification with negative things. They identify with all kinds of petty, negative things in life just as those poor hostages in Stockholm or the Middle East began to identify with their terrorist captors.

Become extremely conscious of what you say out loud and what you allow other people to say out loud to you. Remember that we are programming each other's computers. There's no filter on that computer, either—or else that Stockholm Syndrome would not be true.

A few years ago I went to a seminar in Kansas City. It was one of those where you register at 8:30 and the classes begin at 9:00. Another local psychologist heard I was going down and called to ask if he could ride with me. I'd never met him, but I knew him by name so I agreed. We decided to avoid a night's lodging and save a little money by leaving the morning the classes were to begin—probably not the best decision I've ever made. It takes four hours to get to Kansas City, and this was in the winter.

We started extremely early in the morning and it was very, very dark on the interstate. We hadn't gone more than 30 or 40 miles down the road when I noticed that my companion was saying a number of really very negative things. I thought he should know better, because he's in the business and should know that what he says really does make a difference to others.

"Come on," I said to him. "The last four or five things you've said have really been very negative. I feel good about going to this workshop, and don't want any negative suggestions in my thought process."

Boy, did he get puffed up! I'm not exaggerating when I say that he sat there all puffed up and did not say one solitary word—he didn't even grunt—all the rest of the way to Kansas City. When we finally got to the meeting, he got out of the car, reached in the back seat and got his suitcase, closed the door, and walked away. He didn't say one word, not even thank you.

Needless to say, I was very surprised that he did ride back with me, because he did have several other options. To be completely candid, he was still a little puffy, but he was very careful that everything he said to me was positive. And that's great! **That's just exactly how I wanted it.**

If someone had a great big bucket of garbage and wanted to come over to my house and dump it in the middle of my living room floor, I would not let him do it. You would be amazed to see how aggressive I would become in getting that person and his garbage out of my house.

Now, if I wouldn't let anyone dump garbage in the middle of my living room floor, why in the world would I allow someone to dump garbage into my computer? It would have an effect on me, on my productivity and my happiness, and indirectly on my family.

It's this kind of awareness that you must develop. **Be extremely conscious of your voice-activated computer—that computer that has no filter on it.**

Even though you're extremely conscious of the pitfalls, you can still get caught. It may happen to you, as it has happened to me.

Not too long ago I was at another convention. This one was in Fort Worth, Texas. I didn't know anyone when I went there, but by the second day I'd become acquainted well enough to be talking with the people I'd sat with at lunch.

I'd ordered a very small meal, thinking to myself that since I had just been sitting around, not burning off too many calories, I really shouldn't be putting too many back in.

The gentleman across the table from me asked if I was on a diet. I explained that no, I just didn't need too many calories when I wasn't getting much exercise. And I probably shouldn't have said this, but I added that I have to kind of watch what I eat because I do have a tendency to gain weight.

But bless her heart, the woman sitting next to me, whom I didn't even know, popped right in and said, "Now Ray, don't say out loud that you have a hard time with your weight or you will have!"

So here I am: I teach it, I preach it, and every now and then I get caught at it just like everyone else!

We all need to become conscious of what we say out loud and what we allow others to say out loud to us, for each other's sake as well as for our own. You learn to do it and pretty soon it becomes automatic. The only time you have to really think about something is when you first learn it— afterwards you do it automatically.

Remember when you first learned to drive—all those things going on at the same time and you had to think about every one of them? But now you drive around town automatically, without even thinking about it. **LEARN to do it. LEARN to be conscious of what you say out loud and what you allow others to say out loud to you.**

The process I am talking about is precisely the

method we analyzed earlier in the case of the novice skier. He learned by consciously making many minute corrections in his technique. He employed voice-activation to create mental images. You can use exactly the same techniques to become conscious of input into your mind's computer.

You must create the desire and ability to reverse negative comments as second nature—a conscious, fully internalized belief—if you wish to be successful in overriding negative input into your computer. The negative person is successful in bringing you down to his level because, for whatever reasons, he truly owns those negative beliefs. You must have an equally firm possession of your positive viewpoint.

When someone's input towards you, verbal or otherwise, has been less than positive, there is no reason to assign blame. **If you have made a commitment to like and accept yourself, you can easily accept others the way they are. If you have chosen to be all that you can be, the power of your commitment will overwhelm any negative input.**

Affirmation is the powerful verbal tool by which we develop and maintain self-esteem in both ourselves and others. Positive statements are communicated to the subconscious mind, where they are recreated in the form of images. **Especially when affirmations are stated in the present tense, as if the results you desire already exist, this verbal reprogramming of your belief system is an effortless means of learning constructive behavior.** Use positive verbal programming to validate yourself and others daily.

Notice that in all of these episodes, when a reversal of a potentially negative situation is mandated, they are somewhat akin to our earlier discussion of failure. They are crises—occasions when negative input is assaulting your voice-activated computer. Unless you act to override the negative, your outlook and self-esteem can potentially falter.

But remember that there is nothing inherently wrong with failure. **When failure is experienced with awareness and used as an opportunity for correction, it is an experience in one's quest for success.** As Henry Ford said, "Failure is the opportunity to begin again more intelligently." Add awareness to experience and you get success. Self-esteem is validated when failure brings us closer to the successful solution to a problem or challenge.

Similarly, the reversal and overriding of a negative situation through affirmation validates and reinforces high self esteem in two ways. It ensures that the primary input into our own computer has been positive. And it is a pure experience with success—which creates self esteem.

Like the scientist's or artist's initial failure, these crises of negative input are actually *opportunities*. **There are no solutions, or successes, without there first being problems.** Solving the problem validates self-esteem. Adversity does lead to achievement when it is handled properly. This is the reason why, in the stories of successful people's lives, we so frequently hear of an early difficulty, or trauma that challenged the ultimately successful individual. Triumph over adversity is the essence of success.

The cumulative effect of handling these situations positively alters life patterns. Your **similar repeated experiences become concepts in your mind.** More often than not, experiences are in themselves largely neutral. Going to work in the morning is not an inherently good or bad thing. But your attitude toward it, the self-esteem you bring to the challenge, and what you actually do with the opportunity can be positive or negative. **Both success and failure are equally available, and the choice is yours.**

You always choose to assimilate experiences as positive or negative concepts. Your concepts determine both your level of thinking and your actual thoughts. And we know that the psychosomatic connection means that your thoughts control your performance and your personal happiness. To change your beliefs is to change the consequences that will control your life.

--Utilizing Creative Visualization--

In personal affairs, as in national or world affairs, solutions are achieved through commitment. **Arising out of self-esteem, commitment enables us to persevere through temporary difficulties, understanding them to be corrective operations along the route to successful solutions.**

In *The Healing Brain,* Ornstein and Sobel examine commitment as a characteristic of stress-resistant people. Researcher Susan Kobasa looked at a group of middle- and upper-level AT&T executives during its post divestiture reorganization. Although their backgrounds were similar, the executives were easily divided into high stress/high illness and high stress/low illness groups.

"The psychological hardiness of the high stress/low illness executives was characterized by a strong commitment to self, work, family and other important values, a sense of control over one's life, and the ability to see change in one's life as a challenge rather than a threat. These hardy people accepted the fact that change, rather than stability, was the norm in life and tended to welcome it as an opportunity for growth," wrote Ornstein and Sobel.

In fact, openness to change is so important that it may even prevent cancer! Ornstein and Sobel cite the highly speculative theory of Augustin de la Pena, who suggests that spontaneous, rapidly spreading cancers are promoted by the body's response to information underload (boredom). Says de la Pena: "carcinogenesis is the body's mode of providing 'information-novelty' which is subsequently fed back to the brain and which attempts to rectify the relative information underload signaled by the brain." In other words, cancer cells represent something new to the bored organism.

As you assess your current level of commitment, take a stand in your own life and choose to be all you can be! You choose to take charge of change when you use positive change in the service of your goals. De la Pena's theory suggests that your body positively wants this from you and depends on it for its continued good health. Commitment is a steady vision of one's goals, and commitment is supported and made easier by a clear understanding of the mental processes that govern physical responses.

If you don't know where you are going, any path will take you there . . . and when you get there you'll be surprised. On the other hand, as a wise man once said, "the road called security is marked cul-de-sac or boredom." As we've seen, that may also be the path to life-threatening disease.

When commitment is the road you travel, your destination is whatever goal you have chosen for yourself.

Much of our discussion so far in this book has been devoted to developing an understanding of the mind's functioning—its complete capacity to control actual outcomes through the attitudes and values it holds. We have discussed the human mind's efficient, two-sided division of labor, the significance of its operation by voice-activation, and the psychosomatic connection between mental images and physical responses. And we've explored the complex corrective procedure the brain uses to recognize errors as corrections along its route to a pre-programmed goal.

By now it should be clear that the mind's idea of its goals is of utmost importance. The image the mind has in place governs both all of the mind's other operations as well as consequent physical responses. If the brain has a negative image in place, such as the image of oneself as an overweight person, the language the brain produces will be negative—"I just can't seem to lose weight!"—and the outcome will be consistent with the image the mind holds.

"You are today where your thoughts have brought you—you will be tomorrow where your thoughts will take you," wrote James Allen.

If the mind holds only a fuzzy image of your personal identity, vaguely washing around somewhere in your subconscious, it will make sure that everything you say is bland and that you end up the same way—nondescript.

If you hold in your mind a clear, consistent image of your goal—whatever you seek to achieve, material or spiritual—your brain will cause to happen all of the actions necessary for the outcome you desire.

Your mind will make the necessary changes that will contribute to the goal you seek. The human mind is consistent; it is designed to recognize goals, whether positive or negative, and to follow through to that goal unless instructed otherwise. To change the direction of your life's activity towards a different goal, you need only to change the image you hold of that goal. Then allow your mind to follow through to that end with the commitment that is a natural feature of the human mind.

This positive use of the natural capacity of the human mind is called creative visualization. It is one more technique high achievers characteristically use to maximize their potential. According to Stephen Cates, you too can begin right now to develop your capacity to visualize and to use this technique to recreate yourself as you wish to be. You can live the way you wish to live, accomplish the goals that are important to you, and obtain the personal or material satisfactions you seek. You can learn to expand your expectations, and in doing so you will expand your possibilities.

"Once you expand your mind with a thought, it can never go back to the same dimensions," said Oliver Wendell Holmes.

Creative visualization is not a new or unproven technique, nor is it mysterious or only available to an initiated few. Everyone uses this power because it is a part of normal, ordinary brain function. It uses the two faculties, imagination and visualization, that we have seen to be characteristic of right brain activity.

Typically, however, we don't use these right brain functions consciously, with purpose and direction. You will recall that the right side is the brain's silent half. It apprehends without words, spatially and emotionally, and its steady, frequently creative operation is easily drowned out in our consciousness by a constant stream of intelligent, logical chatter produced by the brain's left side.

Emphasis on left brain activity to the exclusion of right brain function is reinforced by our culture. The left brain's emphasis on language, calculation, and logic matches our culture's orientation towards a linear and sequential perception of reality. So, early on in life, children are reprimanded for "daydreaming," and later on we are discouraged from taking an "intuitive" approach to problems that should be tackled logically and systematically instead.

To use only one side of your brain is to severely restrict your potential. As visualization teacher Cates points out, if you were able to use only one side of your body, you would be defined as handicapped. To use only the left side of your brain is to similarly handicap your mental capacity.

Remember the nature of the brain's typical operation. It translates language input from the left side into right side images that subconsciously control physical response. Mental images are a necessary component of meaning and understanding, and the mind cannot operate without them. The mind will supply whatever images it needs to complete the circuit of understanding and action.

When you allow negative input to enter your voice-activated computer, your mind will supply images that correspond. When you ignore the right side of your brain and allow any arbitrary image to impact on it, your brain will supply a corresponding set of incomplete, fuzzy images to form there. You will wind up going nowhere.

But when you begin using your imagination productively, by vividly and consistently stating and imagining the goals you desire, your mind will efficiently complete the circuit it was designed to perform, producing the outcomes you desire.

There need be no limits to the human imagination. If your imaginative capacities are constrained through force of habit, you can unlock your full creative potential through practiced access to this part of normal mental activity. We will explore some specific techniques for developing positive and creative mental attitudes in later sections of this book. Be assured that these capacities are available to you—no matter what your background or current situation in life may be—because these approaches are based solely on the ordinary pattern of mental activity we all share.

This is a journey to freedom. It is the freedom to choose your own goals and to assume total responsibility for yourself. It is the freedom to recreate yourself in whatever way you wish. Once your goals are entirely your own, the weight of resentment will fall away. You will recognize that resentment arises only out of expectations—the expectations you have had that others will solve your problems, fix it all up for you—and the expectations of others that you once confused with your own goals.

Now hope can replace resentment in your life. "Hope represents a special type of positive expectation," write Ornstein and Sobel. "Unlike denial, which involves a negation of reality, hope is an active way of coping with threatening situations by focusing on the positive."

You, and you alone, must decide between resentment and freedom. If you are now or have been resentful, assuming responsibility for yourself will complete a forgiveness process towards those you have resented. Know this—your freedom will also release someone else.

Freedom doesn't exist until you choose it. But once you have made the choice, the route is clear. **Here, for once, the road is plainly mapped—take the path marked "commitment."** Along the way, make changes in yourself joyfully and willingly, in the service of your goals.

Begin the journey now.

PART TWO:
Thirty *Perfect* Days

You can acquire or eliminate any habit in **thirty perfect days.** Understanding and accepting this exciting and helpful concept has helped me improve my life.

Now if you are a technical person, the numbers actually range from eighteen to thirty days, with the average being twenty-one days. I like to use thirty days because that includes everyone.

The reason most people have a difficult time in changing a habit is because they will stay with their new habit all week and then on the weekend they do something different. Doing this destroys the creation of the new habit. This means that you must stick to the program you've established for yourself for thirty days, **WITH NO EXCEPTIONS!**

If, for example, you decide to get up at 6 a.m. each morning, you must do it every day for the next thirty days—including weekends and other days when you might not otherwise have to get up at 6 a.m. After thirty days, you will automatically wake up at 6 a.m. every morning just as though an alarm clock had rung. And you will feel refreshed and be completely unable to imagine why there was ever a time when you did not get up at 6 a.m.

Or, if you decide to stop eating between meals and you actually do that for thirty perfect days—with no exceptions—you will discover that your mind will validate your new behavior. In fact, seeing someone else eating between meals will immediately trigger the thought that they shouldn't be doing it!

That's it. That's the whole program!

It works because the conscious mind operates in the service of the subconscious mind. The conscious mind is just not as smart as the subconscious mind. But it's the conscious mind from which we operate 95 to 97% of our waking day.

The conscious mind has only two jobs—to keep you doing the same thing over and over again, and to justify anything you do. But it's not smart enough to come up with a real idea of its own. That's the job of the subconscious, visualizing part of your mind. And it takes a little time—eighteen to thirty days to be exact—for the subconscious mind to retrain its servile and subversive partner.

Here's how it works.

Let's say you've decided to lose 10 pounds. The subconscious mind gets that idea in place and develops a good image of yourself in that new way. So you spend the whole day eating small meals, avoiding snacks, and generally doing very well.

When you come home from work, your habitual, conscious mind sends you right to the cupboard—because that's what you always do when you come home from work. But because you've made this decision, your subconscious manages to get your attention and you can tell yourself,"I really don't want anything out of the cupboard. I want a slim, trim, healthy body." So you sit down to read the paper.

Well, since habit didn't work, your conscious mind tries the justifying approach. There are some cookies in the cupboard—and they're your favorite kind.

So the conscious mind will start in on you: "Oh, you've done so well today—no snacks, and you're not even hungry! You know, it's not that you're really hungry, but you do enjoy the taste of those cookies. You could satisfy your urge for the taste of those cookies with just one little bite. You know you won't eat any more because you're not even hungry." And pretty soon you do it—you accept the justification and you go pinch off just one tiny bite of your favorite cookie.

Well, you know the rest . . . "just one bite" turns into "just one cookie" which turns into "just the cookies, nothing else" and in the end, you're lucky if you can get out of the kitchen without cleaning out the whole cupboard.

Thirty perfect days requires that you not allow the conscious brain to subvert your desire with habit and justification during that period. It requires a few days of discomfort. Discomfort is, after all, the price of forming new habits.

As your thirty days progress you'll notice that discomfort quickly subsides. Your conscious mind begins to learn the new habit and learns to justify it instead of its former behavior. And what we frequently see at the end of thirty days is a complete reversal—the reformed smoker, for example, who proselytizes and coughs conspicuously when anyone lights up.

This book is designed to give you the necessary psychological support through thirty perfect days.

There are 30 illustrations with accompanying essays, which are designed to focus on the incredible power of your mental computer in exactly the way it naturally operates. Read these essays right now as an exercise in improving your conscious awareness of the way in which your mental activity governs your behavior. Then, whenever you wish to substitute a new, constructive behavior for a formerly negative habit, return to the essays and read one each day as reinforcement for your program of thirty perfect days.

You are now in the position to put the conscious, verbal left side of your brain in the service of the subconscious, visual right side of your brain. This powerful synthesis will prompt actions that will support whatever dreams and goals you imagine. This will be a dramatic step forward in recreating the person you really want to be.

R E L A X... and let your brain *create* the solution

T here is nothing like a problem to divide the positive people from the negative ones. The problem looms up like the Continental Divide, a great watershed, where you'll find the negative people milling around in the deepest valley. You'll find the **positive people** on the other side, already having scaled the mountain.

When the problem, or mountain, looks pretty big, negative people try to justify their attitudes—all their preconceived notions about why the problem shouldn't be tackled. And, of course, as they speak their justifications aloud, the input into their mental computers merely serves to validate the negative attitudes they already hold.

On the other hand, **highly functioning, positive people look beyond the problems and see several possible solutions.**

Of course, that's not to say that very positive people ignore problems. In fact, typically they're quite good at sizing up the nature and dimension of a problem. But their minds automatically leap to working out the necessary solution. **They actually comprehend a problem in terms of its solution.**

Highly functioning people do not necessarily solve problems immediately. But the very positive person, whose mental images portray him overcoming difficulties, knows how to relax and allow the subconscious mind to take over problem-solving.

You've seen the mind handle small problems in exactly this way. For example, you've probably had the experience of drawing a complete blank when you try to think of a certain person's name. You think: "Oh, gee. I know that name. Just a minute. Leave me alone. Just let me relax and it will come to me." And it is when you back off and relax that the name will come to you.

Permit your mental computer to solve more difficult problems in precisely the same way. It may take two weeks

or two months for your mind to arrive at a conclusion. You
may be taking a shower or you may wake up in the middle
of the night. The answer you unsuccessfully sought when
you consciously pondered the problem will eventually come
to you in a relaxed moment—provided you have maintained
a positive attitude. By being open to positive, helpful input
you will have given your mind what it needs to work on a
solution.

The mind wants to come up with a solution. Once it
understands the problem in a solution oriented way it will
not stop working for you until it comes up with the answer
you need. That is how the mind's mechanism works. It
needs to complete the mental circuit triggered by the
informational input.

Once you start complimenting your own mind for
being an extremely effective problem-solver, it will learn to
love solving problems for you. Emotionally, it will embrace
an attitude of deriving pleasure from solutions. Your
computer loves to work for you on the basis of whatever
attitudes you hold.

Solution oriented people love solving problems even
more than they love solutions. **"Being at the top of the
mountain, or top of anything is not particularly
interesting, but the process of getting there is,"**
says champion mountain climber Gwen Moffat.

Voice-activation prompts both positive and negative
attitudes. Rather than telling yourself "this is a mess," say,
"I always master a situation like this by breaking it down
into manageable parts and approaching each part
systematically."

Brainstorming is a particularly good technique for
generating solutions when responsibility for the issue is
shared by members of a group. It eliminates or reverses
negative input while generating a great deal of positive,
solution oriented input into our mental computers' evaluating
mechanism. Brainstorming is an ideal technique for the
workplace. Fortunately, it works equally well on an

individual, "do-it-yourself" basis.

The ground rules for brainstorming are quite simple. Within a short period of time, usually 15 minutes, as many ideas or solutions as possible are produced by the group. Far out ideas are encouraged, as they may trigger other ideas for someone else. Criticism or evaluation of the ideas is suspended until after the brainstorming session is completed. Then ideas can be evaluated, combined, discarded and ranked.

If the problem is "this is broken," solutions such as "try some glue," "maybe we should call a plumber," and even "let's throw it at the wall and see if it starts working again," constitute effective brainstorming and are equally useful input towards triggering an effective solution.

Comments like "you're the one who broke it" and "maybe the boss won't notice if we don't say anything" serve no solution oriented purpose and may indeed provoke negative images that interfere with the mind's natural ability to work through to a solution.

Blame and resentment are terrible impediments.

Like individuals, groups of people who must work together can train themselves to become solution oriented. There is no room for justification of negative attitudes when the peer group values solutions.

BECOME CONSCIOUS OF HOW YOU CHOOSE TO SOLVE YOUR PROBLEMS!

**When problems arise in your life,
are you prepared to
*"retool?"***

A few years ago, I was working on a housing development project. When it came time to locate financing for a portion of the work, I quickly discovered that all the usual sources of financing had suddenly dried up. Nationally, interest rates were very high at the time, and Nebraska had a legal cap on the rates allowed.

My project was a good one, and under ordinary circumstances I would have had no trouble obtaining the necessary financing. Because of the situation in Nebraska, I had to travel out of the state to arrange the financing. I made a trip to Des Moines, Iowa to look into a possibility there.

While there I happened to meet a gentleman who really put the whole situation into perspective for me. This man was also in the real estate business, so our conversation naturally led to the reason for my trip. In explaining my situation to him, I said that "things were really shut down" in Nebraska.

He listened to me and just smiled. "I know, Ray," he said. "Isn't that *great*?"

I looked at him and said, "What do you mean, 'great'?"

He said, "*It's a wash!*" And then he went on to explain, "This will wash all of the people who don't belong in the business out—and then you and I can get back to making money again!"

In recent years, it's seemed that the entire country has been going through a "wash." This wash has spread through the automobile, steel, oil, and agriculture industries like a cancer invading one organ of the body after another. The human toll of hardship for decent, hardworking families has been, of course, very sad. But the wash itself, a rather violent transformation of these industries with a fair number of corporate casualties, is a good thing—a necessary thing!

In each of these industries, there was a mandate for change. For a variety of reasons—probably different in each case—the situation in these industries got so bad that it was impossible to go on doing things the same old way. The companies involved started to collapse under their own weight. We're still seeing the results, and it's a crisis, much like a failure in an individual's life.

Potentially, it was a very negative state of affairs. When we're faced with adjusting to change a crisis situation often develops. **But there are those who saw this crisis as an opportunity for correction or reversal. Those were the high achievers, the solution-oriented people. They saw the opportunity in the problem.** And, importantly, because they didn't waste any time complaining about the problem, they saw the opportunity before the competition did.

Back in the seventies in Detroit, when the auto industry was hit the hardest, some of those most adversely affected were the owners and employees of the smaller manufacturing companies that supplied parts to the Big Three automotive companies. In retrospect, we can easily see that their mistake had been one of tying themselves too closely to a single customer.

Today the survivors among those smaller companies are the ones who recognized the problem quickly, found new markets, and rapidly changed their equipment or "retooled" to provide different parts to different industries. Today they're more diversified. They created an opportunity for success out of adversity.

They retooled.

That's a good word for what we're talking about here—a response to problems and the inevitability of change. When problems arise in your personal life, business life or social life, are you prepared to "retool"? Are you prepared to be innovative, open to new approaches, and go for the solution rather than to blame, dwell on the difficulty, and justify your inaction?

I live in a farming state, and, as we all know, agriculture is having a crisis of its own right now. Part of the problem for farmers is that they just got too good at doing their job. Irrigation, more effective fertilizers and insecticides, and bigger machinery have led to bigger yields in cornfields all across Nebraska. When the demand isn't there, prices for farm products become depressed. This is an oversimplification of the problem, but I'm not too concerned with analyzing it.

The point is that periodically there is a problem, and I'm interested in the solution. Some farmers will continue to come out of the wash with a new and better way of farming. For them the crisis will be an opportunity. And when they look back and say, "that was the turning point," they'll have the satisfaction and additional self-esteem of knowing that it was a turning point of their own making.

"What is important is not that you have a defeat but how you react to it," says Italian film director Lina Wertmuller. "There is always the possibility to transform a defeat into something else, something new, something strong."

Historically, the agricultural economy affects hundreds of little towns across the farm belt.

And in the midst of this crisis in the agricultural economy, you see a big difference from town to town. There are positive towns and there are negative towns. There are towns with economic development councils and newspapers full of forward-looking editorials, and there are towns full of bitterness, gloom and nostalgia for the good old days.

The bitterness and the blaming are bad enough, but the nostalgia is even worse. No matter how pleasant our memories of the past may be, the reality of the present is change and the opportunities it presents. Whatever your particular situation may be, your happiness and productivity will increase as you live less in the past and more in the now.

**We can focus on any aspect
of our experience,
either positive or negative.**

Three

Inner vision—our mental capacity to visualize imaginatively—is somewhat like actual physical vision, the function our eyes perform. Focus is an important aspect of the process. When we focus visually, our eyes coordinate and locate a particular object in our field of vision, fixes upon it, and it becomes the object of our concentration.

We focus mentally in much the same way. **We can imaginatively scan our entire experience, and we can choose to focus on any aspect of it, positive or negative.** If someone has a bad knee, he can choose to focus on the bad knee or the good knee. If someone has had a particularly difficult weekend, he can choose to focus on the bad weekend or on the many other good weekends he has experienced. In fact, because the imagination's capacity is limitless, he can even choose to focus on plans for a weekend that has not yet occurred.

A man wakes up in the morning. He lives in a beautiful home. Everyone in his family is there—safe, well, and secure. He showers and the water temperature is perfect. He goes down to the kitchen, makes coffee, and it's delicious. When he goes out, he's dressed in nice clothes, he gets into a new car, and drives to work. As he pulls into the parking lot, he discovers that someone has parked in his usual place. And he just comes *unglued!*

By focusing on the single negative in a long series of positive circumstances, this individual is choosing unhappiness. The option to focus instead on any one of the positive things was equally available to him.

In fact, as outside observers, we would probably say that he had "lost perspective." Notice there's another visual analogy in that phrase. **When we put a single bad experience in its proper context among many positive experiences, its importance is definitely minimized.** It takes on the dimensions of a surmountable inconvenience rather than the proportions of an overwhelming problem.

Use your imaginative focus constructively. Really become conscious of the good things—of how lucky you are, of how well things are going for you, because what you concentrate on is what will be attracted to you.

You've heard this expression many times. Good luck attracts good luck. Yes, that's true. Or, money attracts money. Yes, that's true also.

The phenomenon of the self-fulfilling prophecy causes this kind of attraction to occur. Positive mental images and constructive mental processes allow one to be open to the opportunities that are always available.

The aging process is a wonderful example. Have you ever wondered why some people appear old when they've barely reached middle age, and why others seem able to maintain youthful attitudes and activities despite far more advanced years?

No, it isn't "all in the genes." Attitude and mental focus are far more significant factors.

If you have friends who are approaching age forty, you will frequently see a great surge in their focus on age. Forty seems to be a critical age, perceived as a turning point by many people. I believe that forty is the age when experience and potential coincide to enable maximum productivity. But many people see forty as an end, with only a long downhill slide towards infirmity and death ahead.

I've seen people actually celebrate their fortieth birthday with a kind of mock funeral. Everyone wears black, "just as a joke." Humorous gifts include hair dye, laxatives, large print books and wrinkle cream.

Humor is often a mask for our greatest fears. In this situation we see a very negative underlying attitude.

Recently I heard about a woman who took a different approach to the occasion. She invited her friends to her lakeside cabin for a weekend "conference on friends and aging." Guests were instructed to bring a favorite poem about friendship, a list of the five happiest events of the past year, and a list of ten goals for the next ten years.

Guess what?

Everyone had such a good time that they all agreed to get together again a year later.

Turning forty—or fifty or sixty or any age—is an experience the vast majority of us will eventually share. Whether the occasion is a funeral or a turning point towards new potential is—like every other event in life—a matter of where we choose to focus and concentrate our attention.

BECOME CONSCIOUS OF USING YOUR POSITIVE MENTAL IMAGES.

Attitude . . . the *magic* word!

Four

W e automatically want to raise our children to be positive people. We automatically want to be around and have positive people as our friends. We automatically want to believe positive people.

We implicitly believe that positive people are associated with positive outcomes. *Attitude* **is the psychosomatic connection, the magic word.**

Not too long ago, I was riding from Omaha to Lincoln, Nebraska with a friend. All of a sudden a front tire blew out.

He pulled over. I was still a little bit surprised and thinking about what was going to happen next, when he said, "Ray, I'll bet you a buck that I can change that tire in five minutes and be back in the car."

Now, he could have cussed the tire company or told me how many miles he didn't have on that tire, or whatever. But his attitude was so good that his mind automatically focused on how expert he was at changing tires.

Yes, he did it in five minutes. Yes, I was delighted to pay him a buck. I like to be around positive people, and you can certainly see why this guy's my friend.

Attitude **is nothing more than a description or characterization of the constant running tape in your mind.** Really become **conscious** of what that tape is saying and then you will know what your attitude really is.

As my friend's experience with his tire indicates, **life's events are not always predictable. But the tape keeps running, and your attitude is constant and reliable. Whatever is running on that tape when something suddenly occurs will determine your approach to the external event.**

Five

People are said to "struggle with their emotions." Some feelings—fear, blame, guilt, shame—well up in their mind and cause them to act in a way they'd rather not.

Or worse, when people seek to deny their emotions, an even more dangerous emotion, resentment, arises out of a conviction that the broken promises of others are the cause of their own problems. **But ultimately, only you are responsible for your resentments, and you must understand that the price of the resentments you hold most dear can lead to mental and physical illness.**

And always the result of negative emotions is inner conflict—it's that sense of being torn between the rational and emotional parts of oneself. And, as we know, this feeling is real, because the human brain contains exactly this division of labor.

But you CAN learn to control your feelings. You can do it by learning to control your thoughts.

Actors know this technique. Many actors will tell you that when they are called on to express a powerful emotion, such as fear or sorrow, they will focus on an incident in their own experience that provoked the emotion that needs to be produced. Their very concentrated thoughts reproduce the emotion and actually cause the physical manifestation—tears or trembling, for example—they wish to depict. Actors speak of this process as "hardly acting," because it's very real. It's the source of the enormous emotional exhaustion many actors feel after a performance.

This actors' technique is a skill. It's taught in acting schools. It can be learned and developed. You can learn to do the same thing.

Of course you're not interested in learning to feel frightened or miserable. **But learning to be successful is also a skill that you can develop. Being happy is a skill.** These skills are learned in precisely the same way—by using thoughts to produce the corresponding emotions and beliefs.

High self esteem and happiness are the emotions that correspond to success. And a higher degree of self esteem starts the day you start feeling good about yourself.

To trigger it you need only to begin to communicate positive mental pictures of yourself, verbally and visually, to the seat of emotions in the right side of your brain.

Just consider the freedom that is available to you once you recreate yourself in this process. **You—and no one else—have complete control over the images you visualize. You—and no one else—may erase the customary constantly running tape in your head and switch over to something completely different.**

You can range through your entire experience, seeking out past successes—the compliments that meant most to you, exceptionally happy times. You can describe and visualize the future in the most extravagant terms you choose.

Learn simply to enjoy the process of your imaginative potential once again. For many of us, it has been all too long since we truly permitted our imaginations to run completely wild.

We've forgotten what imagination enabled us to do when we were children, but take a lesson from them. Watch a child closely as he or she contemplates riding a bike without training wheels or going off the diving board into the deep end of the pool for the first time. Look at that child's eyes, because there you'll see a glimpse of the visions inside that child's mind. And that child's head will be cocked, as though he's listening to something you can't hear. It's that tape running inside his head. Then, as the mental image is set, you can almost see that little boy or girl nod agreement. Watch closely now: you'll see success happen. And the exhiliration is contagious, enormous enough to sweep *even you*—jaded by experience as you are—right along.

Too often we adults constrain our goal-setting. We think it mainly involves calculations, outlines, flow-charts, and profit and loss statements. Of course these are only measurements of progress and achievement. They are merely steps along the way, not goals in themselves.

Begin again to use your imagination productively. Set no limits. Engage in the process however you please, with verbal instructions to yourself, or with wordless, imagined pictures. Make a commitment to go through the process, and find the infinite freedom available to you!

BECOME CONSCIOUS OF HOW YOU SEE YOUR FUTURE AND YOUR POTENTIAL.

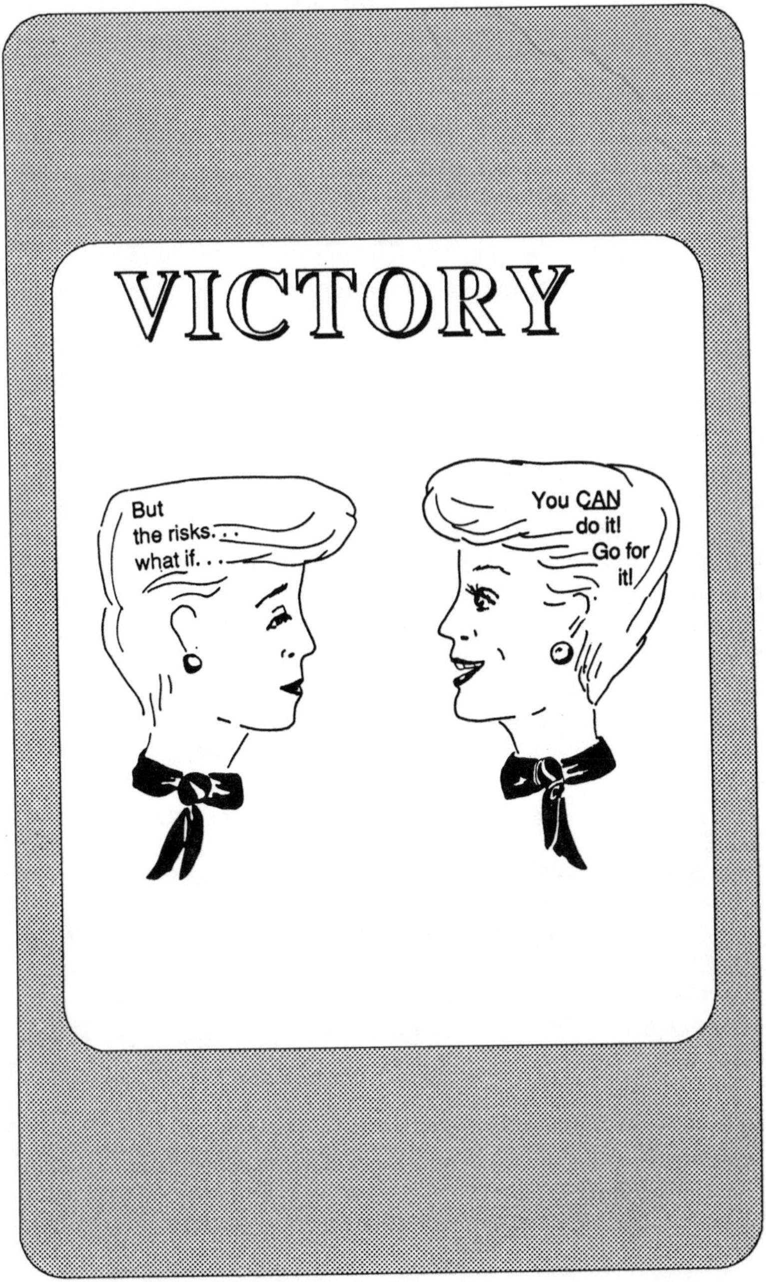
VICTORY
But the risks. . . what if. . .
You CAN do it! Go for it!

Six

T hree prophetic, funny little words:
But what if . . .

You should listen for them in ordinary conversation—other people's and your own. They're the most important prediction you'll ever hear of what's about to happen next.

Take, for example, the office where a new computer system is about to be introduced. If the workers complain:

"But what if it's so complicated that everything takes us twice as long as it does now?"

You can be certain that this is exactly what the outcome will be. But how different the result would be in an office where the employees speculate:

"But what if we could find a way to use this computer to streamline the inefficiencies in the billing system that drive us crazy every month?"

Those three little words herald every justification for resisting change. Those same three little words are just as capable of announcing every dream, imaginative idea or beautiful creation human beings can accomplish. What follows "but what if . . ." is always entirely your option. You can imagine the worst case scenario and express every conceivable reservation or objection . . . or you can envision a future of limitless possibilities, better than today. It's completely up to you. *We literally talk ourselves into and out of every victory in life.*

BECOME CONSCIOUS OF THE LIMITS YOU PLACE ON YOURSELF WITH WORDS SUCH AS WHAT IF, OUGHT TO, SHOULD HAVE, ETC.

**ENTHUSIASM
IS
CONTAGIOUS!!

Seven

Remember the magic word?

Well, "attitude" may be the magic word, but my favorite word is a special kind of attitude:

ENTHUSIASM ! ! !

What a word! What a great word!

Enthusiasm is so important that it should be taught in our schools. And then it should be taught again in our universities.

Oh, yes! Make no mistake about it. Enthusiasm, like any other attitude, is a skill. It can be learned.

Yet some people seem to have a hard time accepting this fact. We want very badly to believe that enthusiasm is some kind of natural characteristic, one that a person is born with or without—like having blue eyes or brown. And so, frequently, you will hear someone say in all seriousness, "I'm just not an enthusiastic person."

And I say, *baloney!* It's just not true.

If I took a chair and said to you, "Okay. If you get up on this chair and act enthusiastic for three minutes, I'll give you a thousand dollars," I guarantee that you'd have my thousand dollars. Because you would become very enthusiastic.

Now, if you can control your level of enthusiasm for three minutes, you can control it for as long as you want. And sooner or later it's going to become a habit. **You can LEARN to be an enthusiastic person.**

And once you're enthusiastic, you can teach enthusiasm without depleting your wallet of a lot of thousand dollar bills. Because **enthusiasm** is **extremely contagious!**

Every time I smile I am showing enthusiasm. And, as you know, it is very difficult to resist smiling back at a genuinely smiling person.

You've probably read that eating chocolate triggers an actual chemical reaction in the brain. Substances called *endorphins* are released, and they have the actual effect of making you feel good. That's one of the main reasons why so many of us like to eat chocolate.

Of course, depending on your situation, you may subsequently feel guilty about eating that chocolate. That's when you sneak back for a little more chocolate: your brain remembers that pleasurable endorphin release and would like to overcome the guilt feelings by regaining that sensation. The guilt and the endorphins keep alternating until you've consumed enough calories to feel really depressed.

What does this have to do with our smiling enthusiast? Wouldn't it be nice to trigger that endorphin release without the guilt that follows?

As a matter of fact, smiling releases far

more endorphins from your brain, into your body, than chocolate does. It's just exactly the same chemical reaction, producing the same good feeling—only more so.

Besides, the nice thing about a smile is that there are absolutely no calories in it!

A smile is the outward, physical manifestation of an interior, mental attitude—enthusiasm. You can prompt the inner attitude by practicing the outer sign of it. Go ahead and try it right now.

Go look at yourself in the mirror and tell yourself "I really like you" five times. I guarantee you'll start smiling before you get that out five times. And you'll genuinely start to feel good, because those smiles are really virulent, extremely contagious. You'll actually reinfect yourself with more enthusiasm.

Medical interns and residents—who know a little about contagious conditions—have a saying: "learn one, do one, teach one." It refers to how quickly they're expected to master new surgical techniques and medical procedures.

Enthusiasm is a skill, and it can be transferred from one person to another in just the same way. Once you've learned it, you'll do it. And once you do it, you'll be teaching it to someone else. Enthusiasm is a great equalizer.

BECOME CONSCIOUS OF HOW ENTHUSIASTIC YOU ARE!

**When you become fully conscious of the
constantly-running tape
in your head, then you are in a position
to improve its content.**

Eight

"**H**e's a **natural** athlete."

"It's perfectly **normal** to be nervous before an important interview."

"You can't expect her to swim as well as her brother—boys are just **naturally** more athletic than girls."

"It's perfectly **normal** to stop for a few drinks on the way home from work - lots of people do it."

What do *you* think about these statements?

Is there such a thing as a natural athlete? To what extent are training and practice factors in athletic performance? Are there certain situations in which it's normal to be nervous? For everyone? Are there natural differences in ability between boys and girls? Is drinking alchohol daily—or ever—normal?

Depending on your experiences, beliefs, and values, you may agree with some, none, or all of these statements. But trying to classify behaviors as "normal" or "natural" will inevitably produce a lot of controversy.

Actually, there is almost nothing that is normal or natural. **There are social conventions, yes. There are habits, yes. But the only thing that is completely natural is the existence of your basic mental equipment, and it is pretty much standard issue for everyone.**

Do the concepts "normal" and "natural" lead you to ideas of personal creativity and potential? Or do you hear cautions, warnings, and justifications when you consider these ideas?

Each of us is self-employed and we work for a company called ME, INCORPORATED. Each morning as you look in the mirror as you shave or comb your hair, you are actually having a Board of Directors meeting. The content of your thoughts and mental pictures during that meeting will have a tremendous impact not only on your day, but in the creation of the rest of your life.

As you proceed through your daily activity, your self-talk is a constant companion. It is a partner—capable of reinforcing your best efforts, but equally capable of rationalizing. Your self-talk can provide you with a myriad of excuses about "normal" and "natural" that justify the status quo.

Your constantly running computer tape's sole function is to interpret for you. It sees events and circumstances in the outside world and explains them to you. It observes you, too, and fits your behavior back into its interpretation. The tape running inside your head seeks to make all things consistent. Become extremely conscious of that tape—its contents and its motives.

It's as though you're having a difficult time with your backhand in tennis. Let's say that's a difficult stroke for you. Before long your opponents will be hitting all their shots to your backhand.

But then, as you become increasingly aware of the problem, you decide to work on it. You practice, you take lessons, and before long your backhand will be your best stroke.

When you become fully conscious of the computer tape running in your head, you will find yourself in a position to program it. You can improve the content of that tape in just the same way you improve your tennis backhand—through awareness, followed by work, practice, and study.

Awareness shatters the meaning of "natural" and "normal" in your life. What's so natural about over-eating or smoking? Since when is it normal to be shy or lonesome or sarcastic? Your tape's content is critical to your potential for success in life. You don't just stumble into success, happiness, and enthusiasm—not any more than you stumble into a good tennis backhand.

Success, happiness, and enthusiasm are skills you can learn. The tape that runs constantly behind your forehead will determine your approach to acquiring these skills for living.

Begin change by becoming conscious of what it's saying.

BECOME CONSCIOUS OF WHAT GOES ON DURING YOUR DAILY BOARD OF DIRECTORS MEETING.

**To model for each other
and our children is the most
important thing we do here on earth.**

Nine

Personal transformation is not an event we experience once in life. Our goals, and the terms that define achievement, change in relation to the situations we create and the circumstances we encounter.

Self-development is not a project one undertakes on a single occasion and then completes once and for all. It can never be considered over and done with. Self-development is a lifetime program.

As we go through life, some measures of our progress are purely internal. The milestones are individual—one graduates, takes a first job, moves on to other accomplishments. These are the achievements that satisfy our human need for self-appreciation and self-respect.

But, let's face it! When we evaluate our lives and achievements, not all measures of success are individual. Listen carefully as you talk to people about what they consider to be their accomplishments and the goals they hold for the future. You will hear a great deal about relationships— about happy marriages, long friendships, and strong family ties. People are deeply concerned about their personal relationships. **Just as human beings have a need for high self esteem, they have an equally strong need for companionship, for friendship, for love, for recognition and for admission into the community of mankind.**

These two very human needs are equally legitimate. One need not be subordinated to the other. Indeed, a serious mental imbalance will result if a man neglects his family out of a drive to achieve, or if a woman suppresses her desire to achieve in pursuing her need for love and family affiliation. Yet this imbalance is frequently the pattern in our society, largely because of artificially limiting distinctions made between male and female "character."

Individual achievement and committed personal relationships are complimentary goals. Without slavishly seeking to please others, we can function in a way that will benefit those we care most about as well as ourselves.

We each have a very real effect on one another. Whether we are particularly conscious of it or not, we observe each other extremely closely. We constantly provide input—positive or negative—for one another's computers with everything we say. We choose our examples and we choose what kind of role models we will be for others.

As far as I'm concerned, everything in life is modeling. Self-improvement is derived from modeling when you choose to follow the fine example of someone you admire. There is nothing more valuable than a mentor in professional life. Your desire to do what's best for your family and friends demands that you provide a positive, productive model for them as you recreate your own life.

I know a contractor who works right along with his

employees. He is modeling for them, and they are very productive workers. A good manager models for the employees he or she supervises. In doing so, the manager teaches them how to be more productive.

To be a role model for each other and for our children is the most important thing we do here on earth.

In raising our children, we are actually teaching them how to raise our grandchildren. And although your children may be grown, the process continues. When you are eighty-eight years old, you will be teaching your children how to be eighty-eight years old. I don't care if they live across the country—it goes through the air somehow, and modeling is the way it happens.

Modeling, like self-improvement, is a lifetime program. The two processes are inextricably tied together, each serving the other synergistically. Together they continue through life, enriching our experience.

**BECOME CONSCIOUS
OF THE KIND OF ROLE MODEL YOU
ARE FOR OTHERS.**

**This is
going to be a
great day!!**

Ten

Since happiness is an interior quality, it only makes sense to say that it must come from within. No one else can make you happy. In fact, if you predicate your happiness on the actions of others, sooner or later you will be let down. If happiness depends on your spouse remembering your anniversary or your boss complimenting you on a job well done, you will eventually face disappointment or resentment.

Blaming others, and living with the resentment that follows, is the single most important cause of unhappiness in the world. Yet resentment is impossible if you accept full responsibility for your own actions and achievements. Assuming full responsibility for yourself means assuming full responsibility for your own happiness.

Resentment follows, too, from mistaken efforts to please others. The person who spends a lifetime in a job he hates just because his family, friends, and society hold that position in high esteem will die a bitter person, seething in resentment and disappointment over what might have been. It may have been a fear of failure or fear of ridicule that prevented him from attempting what he aspired to. But in avoiding temporary disappointment, he chose resentment instead—a far greater misery.

I once met a woman who had fallen in love with and married a man from New Zealand. He wanted to live in his native country, and she agreed to go with him. "Won't you miss your family and your country?" her friends objected. "You'll be giving up all you've accomplished here," they said.

She told me the answer to this, the response she finally worked out and repeated again and again. "I've been happy here, that's true. But I don't believe that there are happy or unhappy places. **I make my happiness for myself wherever I go.**"

**What are *you*
teaching others
about *you*?**

Eleven

The arctic hare, the marten, the silver fox—all those beautiful animals of the snowy northern reaches of our world—mimic their environment, changing their fur color seasonally to reflect the changed appearance of the landscape they inhabit. Tropical birds bear the same flamboyant colors as the lush vegetation that surrounds them. When you look at an animal, you can almost tell from what environment it comes. It's a fascinating phenomenon to reflect upon, a glimpse into the marvelous harmony of the natural world.

Human beings, however, are quite different. Look around yourself—the way your home is decorated, the arrangement of the surface of your desk at work, the contents of your refrigerator, the car you drive. Your environment is a reflection of you.

Really look at yourself. If you were to meet yourself, what would you think?

If someone were to come into the room where you sit right now and just stand there, your mind would go right to work. You would decide so many things about that person—what he was doing there, his occupation, what kind of educational background he has. When he finally did say something, you'd pay a great deal of attention to the words he said, their arrangement, and the tone of his voice—as a way of confirming your impressions.

So many little things give us clues—hairstyles, shoes, the length of a woman's skirt or the cut of a man's suit. You can become very expert at reading the most subtle clues, but the practice is so pervasive that it extends to include the widespread social customs. For example, just think of the number of people you see walking around wearing wedding rings.

It's called *nonverbal communication.* It's a whole range of behaviors from facial expressions, gestures, and posture to all the elements of personal style that communicate attitudes, beliefs, and values every bit as strongly as what a person actually says.

A number of studies have been done on this subject. The study presents a person to a group of people and asks them to evaluate her. Then the same person is presented to a second group—this time dressed in different clothing and using different body language and mannerisms. The evaluation in this case is quite different—even though the person is the same.

Animals live by instinct and genetic coding. They don't consciously or intelligently decide to mirror their environment. But human beings live by their creative imagination. We design ourselves, construct ourselves, write the scripts that recreate our lives.

In my counseling practice people often complained that "he treats me like a servant" or "she treats me like a piece of furniture." And I'd always say the same thing. "I'm curious. What are you doing to teach him to treat you that way?"

When you walk into a room as a stranger to everyone there, you make an statement before you ever open your mouth. You assume the role of a teacher, and what you're doing is teaching everyone in that room exactly how they should treat you.

Stand in front of a full length mirror. Take a good look at the person you see reflected there. How would you treat that person if you were to meet him or her? If you don't like the way others treat you, examine the message you're sending. You're the one who is teaching other people how to treat you.

**BECOME CONSCIOUS OF HOW
YOU ARE TEACHING
OTHERS TO TREAT YOU.**

Twelve

Where I'm from in western Nebraska, we have a lot of coon dogs, and some people remind me of those coon dogs.

Coon dogs have very simple names like Sam or Blue or Charley, and coon dogs always howl. Let's say you're trying to read, and Charley's out there and he's just bellering. You could throw something at Charley, holler at him, and say "hey, Charley, cut it out," but he's just going to continue to beller.

Now if you own a coon dog, you know what you have to do. You have to walk over and pick Charley up by the tail. Sure enough he's sitting on a cockleburr or a sandburr, and you're going to have to pull it out! Then you can set him back down—because he's not going to move—and then he'll be quiet for a while.

Now of course Charley could have gotten up and pulled that cockleburr out by himself. But he never did. I think Charley would just rather beller about it.

You know, some people are like that. They'd rather holler about a situation than do anything to solve their own problems. When I meet someone like that, I just walk up and say,

"Are you a coon dog?"

And if he doesn't know what a coon dog is I'll explain it to him.

It's all right to come right out and really confront that person. Because if you don't, I can tell you right now that it's really going to get on you. It's going into your computer, and the next thing you know you're going to start modeling that coon dog behavior and sharing that coon dog attitude.

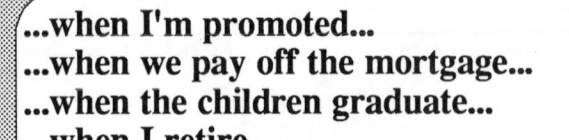

...when I'm promoted...
...when we pay off the mortgage...
...when the children graduate...
...when I retire...

...then I'll be happy!!

Thirteen

I find that so many people are waiting for something. And waiting is no fun! Waiting can make you angry, impatient, frustrated or disappointed. Or maybe it makes you howl like a coon dog.

You meet a little boy who can hardly wait to be a boy scout. "When I get to be a boy scout," he says, "I can go places without my mother." It's as though he believes that happiness begins when he can become a boy scout. You meet this boy later on and he says, "Boy, when I get a driver's license and I don't have to ask my dad to take me places." He thinks, "that's when life begins."

Later, it's when he graduates from college and begins to earn his own money, or when he gets married and has his own family. And the list goes on. When he owns his own home. When he gets transferred out of this lousy town. When he gets a divorce. And finally, when he retires . . . that's when life begins.

Well, you've heard it before, but it's true—there is no tomorrow.

There is only right now, and you'd better find some way to enjoy it. If you're stuck in a traffic jam, you'd better turn on some good listening music or a motivational tape. If you're waiting in the doctor's office . . . pick up a book or plan your next day's activities. Life is only right now, there is no tomorrow.

And when you take good care of right now, I promise you that all of those tomorrows will be well taken care of.

**"Well, that's just
the way I am."**

Fourteen

Are you standing around waiting because you don't want to make a mistake?

Maybe you pride yourself on not being impulsive; you've saved yourself a lot of grief this way. **Maybe right now you're waiting to finish this book before, *heaven forbid*, you try any of these suggestions.** After all, you wouldn't want to make a mistake with something as important as your potential. Right?

That's right, people do make mistakes. Just don't make the biggest mistake of all—doing nothing. If you make a mistake . . . well, that's great. Just never put yourself down for it. Don't validate it and don't justify it. All you have to do is say out loud "I'm not going to do that again!" and go on. That's all it takes to turn your mistakes into the learning steps they really are.

People who attempt to justify their mistakes say many things, but it all comes down to that one statement you hear so often: **"Well, that's just the way I am!"**

What a terrible insult for a person to give himself! When a person says, "that's the way I am," you can bet that person's computer is unplugged on the subject because no new information is going in.

We change all the time. Reflect on it for a minute. You are not the same person you were three years ago, five years ago, seven years ago. Yes, we are changing all of the time. If a person is not changing it truly means she's not growing—not allowing new ideas to go into her computer.

As you recreate yourself, really become conscious of change in yourself and the factors that have caused it—about how change will occur for you now, in the months to come, and far into the future. Recognize that you have control over that change by being extremely conscious of what is going into your computer—that constantly running tape which governs your life.

Develop your hats!

Fifteen

This might be considered blasphemy in some circles, but I really must say that Sigmund Freud, the father of modern psychology, made one fairly big mistake. You know, Freud suggested that we ought to collect all the aspects of ourselves into a single, consistent personality—one grandiose superself.

What a bunch of baloney!

Each of us is ten, twelve, fifteen different people. Now don't worry. I'm not talking about schizophrenia or split personalities. I'm simply referring to the many and varied roles we have in life, and the many and varied characteristics we bring to bear on these roles.

I personally am eleven different people. I know every one of them extremely well—because they're all different, I even like some of them better than others. I haven't created a new person for a long time, but I'm working on one, number twelve. But for now, I'm eleven distinct individuals.

Actually, you can call these personalities anything you want. They're faces, personalities, or **hats. I like to call them my hats.** I carry my hats with me all of the time—I even have them in the shower. I always know which hat I have on, and I can change hats whenever I want to.

For example, let's say I'm a parent with a very young child at the table. As I'm talking to the child, you can tell that I'm a parent by the word arrangement, tone of voice, and body language I use.

Then let's say my wife says something to me. When I turn to answer her, I change. My word arrangement, tone of voice, and body language change, and now I'm a husband.

Then the doorbell rings. It's my neighbor, who wants to borrow a hammer. I'm now an altogether different person again.

There you have three distinct personalities. And I haven't even been out of my house yet.

Now, by and large, I like to go out of my house and wear some of my other hats. But I must admit that one place I go is rather difficult for me. I have a difficult time at large house parties. So I created a person to help me out. This is what I do.

I drive to the party, and as soon as I get in the house, I look for the nicest place for me to sit away from all of the confusion. I go there, and I let this other guy go to the party.

You may meet him some day, because he gets around a lot. But I'll tell you right now, he's phonier than a three dollar bill. He'll go around and shake everybody's hand, put his arm around you, meet everyone in the house. He'll even go into the kitchen to meet the cook. He'll laugh at everyone's jokes, and he'll listen to the same identical joke all over again and laugh just as hard.

I've only got one problem with this guy. He gets invited to too many parties. I never let him drive home. I always drive home. I'm a much better driver than he is.

I'll admit I've got one hat that I make sure I don't wear around other people. It's my bad-ass hat—the one I wear when I'm venting frustration and anger. I don't wear it often, but when I do I always make sure I'm not around other people. And sure, I've got a goof off hat that I wear when I'm lying around on the couch.

But the important thing is that I wear my hats one at a time. When I've got that goof off hat on, I want to make sure that I do a good job of it. It's not going to bother my conscience if I'm just wearing that one goof off hat. It's not going to confuse other people, either. Wearing three or four hats at a time confuses yourself as well as others.

Am I ever bare-headed? To be honest with you, it's really very rare.

You see, I'm very familiar and confortable with my various hats. I've cultivated the personalities they represent, and you should do this too, as you recreate yourself.

You already have these personalities. Identify them. Identify with them. Develop them. By making them distinctive, you will ensure that they come to the forefront one at a time. In this way they will work most effectively for you, and you will be saved the confusion and guilt that arises when they try to perform at the same time.

BECOME CONSCIOUS OF THE DIFFERENT HATS YOU HAVE AND WHICH ONE YOU HAVE ON AT ALL TIMES.

**Without
Order and Discipline...
Life is a *MESS*!!**

Sixteen

The entire universe is governed by the principles of discipline and order. Sun, moon and planets cross the heavens in a reliable, orderly procession. At home on earth the sun rises each morning, and the seasons of the year follow one upon another in an ageless, logical sequence.

The human race survives to the extent that it lives in harmony with these universal principles. **Human beings imitate the order they find in the universe, and in spite of frequent disruptions, human societies are remarkably disciplined and orderly.**

Think, for example of the last time you drove your car. You obeyed the rules of the road without question, keeping to the right side of the road and stopping at intersections and red lights. And your safety depended equally on the other drivers' unquestioning acceptance of the same rules.

Human beings basically like order and discipline so well that they even organize their leisure time activities according to very strict structures. I don't care what sport you enjoy participating in or attending as a spectator—if you think about it, you'll find that the rules of the game are extremely complex. And if you try to imagine the game without any rules, you'll quickly see that it wouldn't be much fun at all.

Sure, we all bristle sometimes under the many rules, systems, and timetables we must constantly submit to. The only alternative to order and discipline is chaos—an unbearable mess. If I allowed myself to do anything I wanted to do just because I wanted to do it, I'd probably be in jail.

That's why the creation of order and discipline in your own life is essential. You won't get home if you don't obey the traffic rules. And you won't achieve your goals if you don't have a systematic plan for achieving them.

Children "want to" have candy bars for supper, and having them might produce instant gratification. But the mature adult rejects the idea of candy bars for supper—no matter how good they might taste—because such a meal would not contribute to good health and appearance.

The difference is that the adult, having attained the age of reason, sees the meal as contributing to a goal that is something beyond immediate gratification. A healthy meal is one step toward a healthy life.

Yet in spite of their more logical minds, adults still lapse into infantile "want to" behavior. Adults may drink, smoke and eat more than they know is good for them. Extramarital affairs are "want to" behavior, and so is the financial difficulty some people run into when they run up enormous credit card bills.

Of course, there is nothing wrong with adults enjoying themselves. A weekend or an evening of pure leisure is regenerative. Making time in our overall schedules for hobbies and relaxation is critical to our mental and physical health. Goofing off is great when it comes at the appropriate time. Then it's part of an overall order and discipline you have chosen in your life. But goofing off is a problem when it comes as a result of not happening to feel like going in to work one particular morning.

The best way to avoid "want to" behavior is to hold your real goals very clearly in mind. Then your mind will naturally weigh each impulse against those goals. That candy bar for supper, that attractive stranger, or that unnecessary expensive luxury will look less appealing in the light of your true goals.

BECOME CONSCIOUS OF THE ORDER AND DISCIPLINE IN YOUR LIFE.

THE CHALLENGE
OF BEING NICE.

Seventeen

The human mind does not tolerate imbalance very well. The mind is always striving to be consistent with the external world, and if it senses that it is out of balance, it will take corrective action to get back in line.

This tendency can be dangerous. It's a big factor in the Stockholm Syndrome and other forms of brainwashing. But we know the mind is pretty indiscriminate—it's just as eager to get back in harmony in a positive way.

This human behavioral trait is the foundation for another hobby of mine. It's a great hobby because the opportunity to practice it comes up all the time, even when I'm right in the middle of doing something else. All it takes is a really unpleasant person.

I know it sounds strange coming from me, but I actually seek out unpleasant people—just so I can practice my favorite hobby.

I developed this hobby about 23 years ago, at the time of a very important change in my life. I'm a very different person now than I was then. So, in order to explain my hobby, I first need to describe how I might have behaved before this hobby became a part of my life.

Let's say that, about 25 years ago, I went into a large department store to buy a billfold. I encountered a salesperson at the billfold counter who was chewing gum, talking on the phone, and otherwise not helping me with my selection. In fact, she actually made me feel I was interfering with her personal phone call!

To tell the truth, 25 years ago I would have reacted by being equally unpleasant. I would have thrown down my money and said something like, "why don't you get a job where you don't have to be nice to people?" And then I would have stomped off, leaving her more unpleasant than I'd found her.

But now I've changed. Today I will go into that same department store and scout out the most unpleasant salesperson I can find. I've even bought things I don't want, just to maneuver myself into position to encounter one of these unpleasant people.

So here I am buying a billfold again. But today I'll tell that salesperson, "Oh gee, this billfold is exactly what I want." And when she hands me my change, I'll touch her hand lightly and say, "This billfold is going to make me so happy—you've really made my day. Thank you!"

Now she's off balance. She's standing back behind her counter thinking, "he's really a pretty nice guy." And that thought is out of balance with the negative view she's had all morning. To get back in balance, she must begin acting consistently with the niceness she's just encountered.

She will want to make it right with you in particular. If, instead of a salesperson, it's the headwaiter in a restaurant you frequent, you will find that you suddenly start to get the best service in town from that person. If it's a co-worker, you will find that you start to get more cooperation and extra effort than you ever dreamed of.

When you engage people in this way, you have accepted the challenge of being nice. And when you have succeeded in communicating change to people, you are entitled to a very proud feeling. You know that you're in control—that you are not permitting a situation to control you.

BECOME CONSCIOUS OF KEEPING
YOUR LIFE IN BALANCE.

The Impact of Communication.

Eighteen

Almost every time there's a problem in our lives it is generally due to a breakdown in communication.

It's so important for us to understand the impact we have on each other by what we say to one another. In order to do that we must first understand the defensive brain and how it works.

Let's say that I'm a school teacher with several children sitting around a table. One little girl, Mary, is all slouched over, and I would like her to sit up nice and straight like the other children. I know I do not dare say to her, "Mary, why don't you sit up nice and straight like the other children?" I know what will happen if I do.

Mary will automatically become defensive, and she will answer with something like, "Oh, teacher, I have a headache," or "I'm tired because I stayed up late last night doing my homework." In other words, I am forcing her to justify and put into concrete a behavior that I'm not in agreement with!

Well intentioned, loving parents sometimes force defensive behavior on the part of their children by their comments about their choice of friends, for example. Remarks like, "You know she runs around with the wrong crowd" or "He's a terribly reckless driver" make it necessary for the youngster to justify their friend's actions. And the justification goes back into the youngster's mind and is accepted as fact.

Do not crowd your loved ones into justifying themselves. What are you supposed to do— just let them do whatever they want to do? No, of course not!

One of the nicest things about people is that all of them slip up and do something right—at least now and then! Watch for those moments! Compliment them on what they're doing right! And then they won't have to justify behavior that you're not in agreement with!

When you get squeezed ... what comes out of you?

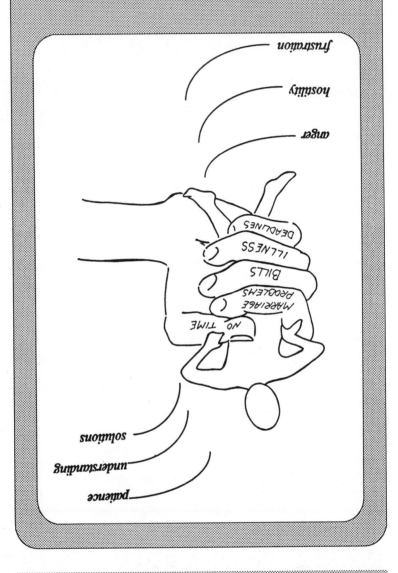

frustration

hostility

anger

DEADLINES

ILLNESS

BILLS

MARRIAGE PROBLEMS

NO TIME

solutions

understanding

patience

If you were to take an orange and squeeze with all of your strength you would get orange juice.

Do you know why you get orange juice? (This isn't an I.Q. test!) Because that's what is inside. Nothing else can come out.

It doesn't matter if you squeeze it in the morning or in the evening—or how you squeeze it— or what month you squeeze it—you're still going to get orange juice. That's what's inside—and that's the only thing that can come out.

I love to watch what happens when a person is squeezed. Now the way you squeeze a person is very similar to squeezing an orange—you apply a little pressure. Pressure like three past due payments, four phone calls on hold, a down computer system or a late arriving plane.

If anger, frustration, indecision and bitterness come out, that's what is inside. If patience, understanding and positiveness come out, that's what is inside. The only thing that can come out is what's inside. What comes out of you when the pressure is on?

Unlike the orange, if you don't like what's inside of you, you can change it.

BECOME AWARE OF YOUR THOUGHT PATTERNS AND WHAT HAPPENS WHEN YOU'RE UNDER PRESSURE.

Twenty

The more you reflect on change, the more you will come to understand it as a critical and essential element in YOUR life. It is pervasive through all aspects of the natural world—including our human nature—and whatever understanding of reality we have is based on our recognition of change.

Change in our lives is a true paradox. Achieving our goals depends on change, and yet it is also human nature to avoid change. The determining factor in our attitude towards change is whether or not we feel we have some degree of control in the changes we experience.

We can activate change in the service of our goals. Through a very active, conscious approach, we can even transform the mistakes and errors we make into learning experiences and positive change.

The change we really dread is broadside change—the accidental and unexpected change that occasionally visits our lives out of the blue. Illness. Accidents. The death of a loved one. Natural disasters. Forced retirement. Our terror of these situations is based in our knowledge that we are not in control of the change. We are temporarily without the control we so cherish.

But the key word is "temporarily." If we survive horrible, unanticipated change, control is instantly returned to us. The next step is ours. And what that next action must be is clear.

We must learn to get up.

Now I am very aware that I have not experienced some of the most extreme tragedies that can befall people. But we all have our share of misfortune in life. In my case, one of the traumas I've experienced has quite literally involved learning to get up.

When I was in third grade, I had infantile paralysis—they call it polio now. That was back in the days when they quarantined the whole family, and it was a very debilitating and even humiliating experience.

As I was recovering, my father would prop me up against the window, and I would look outside at the other children, running and playing. More than anything else, I wanted just to walk without a limp.

Physical therapy was not a developed science in those days, but what was taught as a form of rehabilitation was dancing, toe-ball-heel. So while everyone else was playing football, I was dancing. And I got to be a very good dancer.

Later on, being single and a very good dancer was a real advantage back in the days when ballroom dancing was popular. It was great! I had dates and plenty of partners whenever I went to a dance. I even had the marvelous opportunity to teach dancing on an early Omaha TV show.

This was all going along great, when I just happened to have an accident. It was the worst kind of accident for someone in my situation—I cut off three toes with a lawnmower. Needless to say I lost the TV show and even worse there I was limping again, because you have to have your big toe to walk without a limp.

Yet it was probably the best thing that happened to me in my life. With the dance show gone, I went back to school and got a good education. That accident is probably the only reason why I'm not a dance instructor on some cruise ship today.

I learned to get up. And, you know, I must finally be getting pretty good at this particular kind of getting up. About five years ago, I did it again. This time I ripped the ligaments in my knee in a skiing accident, and again I was in the same situation. It still was very important to me to walk without a limp, and the skiing accident was serious enough to cause permanent damage to my knee.

So I went right back to the toe-ball-heel therapy, just as I'd learned years ago. And today I walk without a limp.

There's a gentleman who has an office upstairs from mine. It happened that he had exactly the same accident just three weeks before mine. And sweat beads break out on my forehead every time I see him coming down the hall. Although he's fifteen years younger than I am he still walks with a limp.

Learn to get up! If you had the privilege of examining the very private side of any individual who has truly excelled, you would probably learn of a significant trauma in that person's life. It's likely that such an individual will not discuss it a great deal—he will prefer instead to emphasize consequential events—his story of getting up.

Tragedy cannot be reversed. But it is possible for something good to come out of tragedy, even though you cannot imagine what at the time. Train your mind to look for the opportunity that is always there!

**BECOME CONSCIOUS OF SEARCHING
FOR THE OPPORTUNITY
HIDDEN IN EVERY CRISIS.**

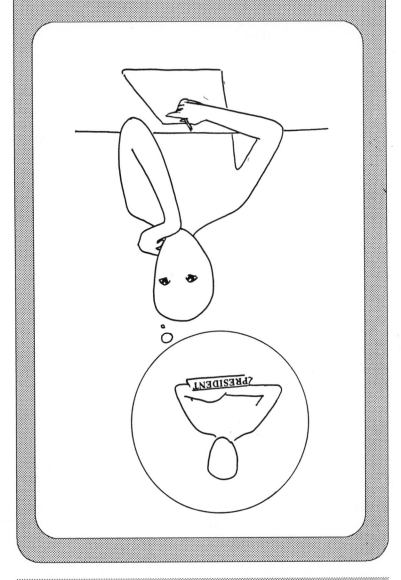

Twenty-One

Scientists have made considerable progress in this century in understanding the human mind. They have looked at it from many angles, including the medical—anatomical, chemical, neurological—and the behavioral—psychological, sociological, and pathological. A lot of the mystery has been removed, and the popularizing of scientific discoveries have given us a lot of opportunity to take greater charge of our mental potential.

One of the ideas that has received a great deal of popular attention is the increasingly accurate mapping of the brain. Scientists have determined that specific areas of the brain are specialized to perform unique functions. It's a very efficient mechanism without a lot of duplication of labor.

One of the most important separations of labor in the brain is between its two sides, left and right. Elsewhere in this book we've described the separate functions of the two sides of the brain and how they interact to complete a purposeful mental circuit, positive or negative.

It's the right side of the brain that produces pictures,

and you cannot think unless you think in pictures. When I say "school," you get a mental image of schoolhouse, school books, teachers, student—you don't see the word "s-c-h-o-o-l" in print unless you deliberately try to think about it that way, say for purposes of spelling it.

Now, this is all very interesting. In fact it's so fascinating that it's easy to get all caught up in finding out all about this, while forgetting the real message contained in this information.

The real message in this information is that there is an enormous amount of potential in a mental process we all share. We all have the capacity to imagine mental pictures—dull ones, mundane ones, and explosively creative ones.

There is credible evidence that these pictures formed on the right side of the brain are the source of inspiration.

We have a little bit of a tendency to think of inspiration as an old-fashioned way of looking at getting certain things done. The ancients were more comfortable with the idea of inspiration—they considered it divine. To us it sounds like something that used to happen to romantic poets; we are far more committed to the "10% inspiration, 90% perspiration" approach. Ours is a very practical age.

But if you listen to highly creative people talk today about how ideas come to them, pretty soon you will start hearing about the pictures or scenes that trigger their thinking. They go on to represent these images in stories or paintings, or they work their "visions" out as scientific formulas or mathematical equations. The Nobel Prize laureate J.D. Watson has said that he worked out just such a mental picture in the process of his discovery of the structure of DNA.

How good are your mental pictures? I'm not suggesting that you necessarily take up biochemistry or start planning your novel, but I am suggesting that highly creative people have exceptionally vivid mental pictures. Surely there are issues in your life that can be better managed by creative thinking.

Begin to think creatively by enhancing the mental pictures you have in mind. Sharpen the focus and fill in the details. Their increased clarity will improve their capacity to inspire you. In later chapters of this book you will learn how to utilize those mental pictures in creating the very proud, productive and happy person you want to be.

BECOME CONSCIOUS OF USING YOUR MENTAL PICTURES TO YOUR ADVANTAGE.

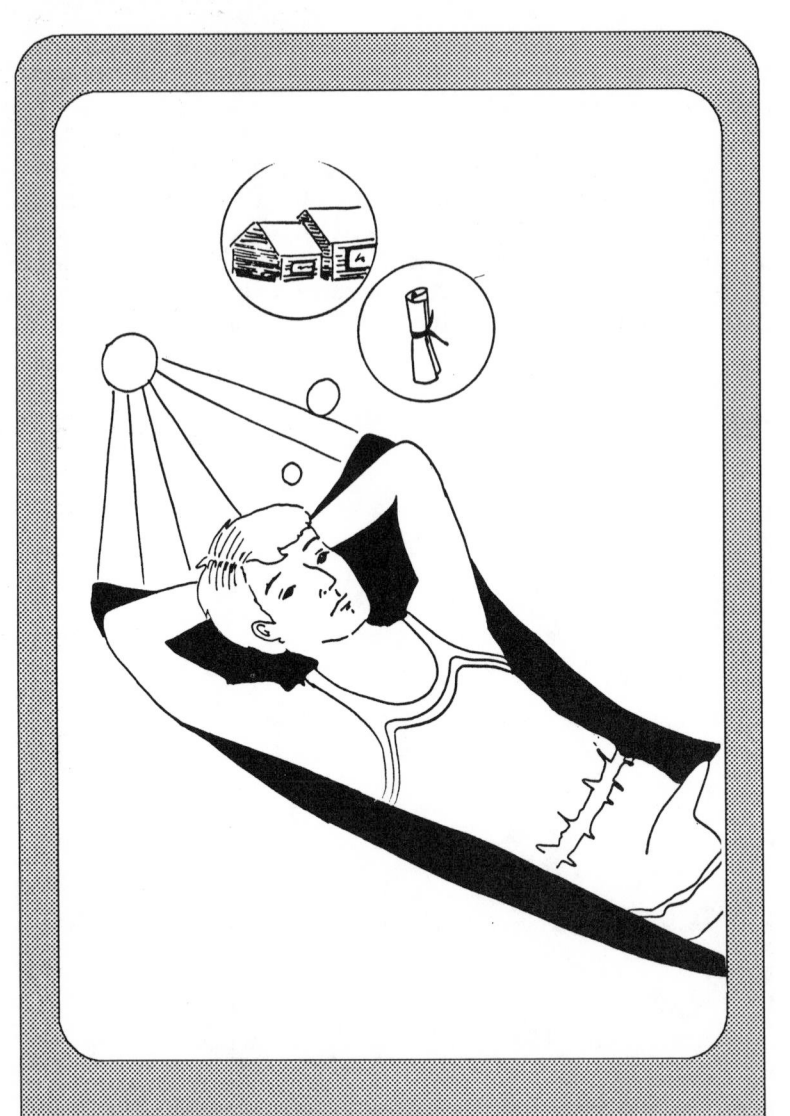

**When your body is unemployed,
your mind should be *employed*!**

Twenty-Two

Sleep, rest, and relaxation are requirements for the body's physical health. Mental relaxation is also necessary for overall well-being, and many of us have become highly aware that physical exercise promotes mental relaxation.

It is important to realize that the reverse should also be true. Important mental activity—mind exercise—should take place when your body is at rest. When your body is unemployed, your mind should be employed.

The absence of physical activity does not mean that you are being idle. Mental activity steps in to replace the physical activity. This is true even while you sleep.

As we sleep, everything that we believe and experience is sorted and reorganized into new mental images that stimulate our waking behavior. This is the activity that we experience as dreaming.

Meditation, contemplation, prayer and visualization are all similar forms of mental activity that can come into play when the body is at rest. These mental activities are in no sense a "waste of time." Rather, they are a highly creative form of activity that will contribute to your self-discovery and help you achieve your goals.

Learn to appreciate and utilize this creative function of your mind as you create your future. Once you recognize and compliment this natural ability it will flourish.

> **BECOME AWARE OF HOW YOU CAN USE CREATIVE MENTAL ACTIVITY TO HELP YOU ACHIEVE YOUR GOALS.**

YOUR MENTAL LIFE
IS
YOUR REAL LIFE!!!

Twenty-Three

Y our mind contains all the necessary, complex apparatus that enables you to be a movie director. And the film you create is a vivid, elaborate documentary of your life—including memories of the past, images of the present, and a scenario for the future.

Across this movie screen inside your mind, images form. Whole stories are told. And all the while a running, verbal commentary accompanies the visual part. It can contain repeated, real dialogue or imaginary conversations. It can be a voice-over narration like the description newscasters read to accompany news footage.

What enormous control you have over these mental movies! You are actor, director, writer, cinematographer, and film editor all in one. If you want to add a musical score, you need only imagine it, and it is there as a full symphony accompaniment—for you have ultimate, complete control over this story, including its outcome.

Make no mistake about the meaning of this power. The endless running tape in your mind is not some Walter Mitty fantasy life. It is not an alternative to reality.

Your mental life IS your real life. It is the place where outcomes are established, where success is determined. The mental pictures and the running commentary we have in our minds is the most important thing that goes on in our lives.

BECOME AWARE OF THE CONTENT
OF YOUR MENTAL PICTURES AND THE
CONSTANTLY RUNNING COMMENTARY
WHICH ACCOMPANIES THEM.

Recreate yourself with your mental pictures.

Twenty-Four

The extremely incredible message of this book is that you act out the mental pictures in your head-AND THERE ARE NO EXCEPTIONS!

Look at the policeman directing traffic on the street corner. Why is he a policeman? Perhaps as a child his favorite story was about a policemann, or his high school counselor once said he would make a good policeman. He started talking about policemen. And as the mental image of a policeman became stronger and clearer, he identified more and more with it, and eventually he became a policeman.

Is there something other than what you are now that you'd like to be? If you can imagine it and if you can believe it, you can make it happen. By forming mental pictures of yourself in the role you desire, you will put in motion the process of becoming exactly the person you want to be.

Remember, we're all in the process of becoming. No matter what your age, it's not too late to choose change. No matter how accustomed you are to your present situation, you need not feel silly or embarassed to imagine something entirely different. The process of self-creation is life long.

When I decided to become a professional speaker I began creating mental pictures of myself as a professional speaker. Then I set out to meet and visit with as many professional speakers as I could. As I learned more about the profession, my mental pictures became even more detailed. I began telling my family and friends that my next occupation was that of a full time professional speaker. And, almost immediately, the doors of opportunity began to open for me. Now I am a professional speaker!

You are a prisoner of the mental images in your mind, held in bondage to them if they are negative. But if you see yourself as a very proud, happy, productive person, you will find yourself dressing the part, talking the part, acting the part, and indeed being the part. The connection is entire and inevitable—whether your mental images are positive or negative.

**Your attitude and mental
pictures
affect your health.**

Twenty-Five

Just as diet and exercise play an important role in determining our health, so do our mental pictures.

Norman Cousins tells of an incident that occured at a football game when four people reported to the First Aid Station with food poisioning symptoms.

The examining physician determined that the only common link among the four was that they had all consumed drinks from a soft drink dispensing machine. An announcement was made to the spectators advising them not to drink drinks purchased from the machines because of a possibility of food poisioning.

Immediately people began fainting and retching. It took ambulances from five hospitals to transport the ill to hospitals. Over two hundred persons had to be hospitalized and hundreds of others visited their private physicians. All had the same symptoms of food poisioning.

When it was finally determined that there was, in fact, nothing wrong with the drink machine, a funny thing happened. People mysteriously began to get well!

If words and mental pictures can make us ill, can they also keep us well? Many physicians now recognize the important connection between body and mind. Remember your mind controls your body. Positive attitudes, thoughts and mental pictures can make the difference between good health and illness.

BECOME CONSCIOUS OF HOW YOUR ATTITUDES, THOUGHTS AND MENTAL PICTURES AFFECT YOUR HEALTH. KEEP THEM POSITIVE!

**Recognize the building blocks
of high self-esteem.**

Twenty-Six

Higher self esteem is the most valuable human quality.

Not only is self esteem the characteristic that determines your productivity, personal happiness, and success, it is also the very best thing you can offer another person. In fact, the greatest gift you can offer another person is a very proud, productive, happy you! It's what others want most from you. Who in the world would want a negative, gloomy friend?

If I were to ask you if you would like your children to have high self esteem, you would certainly answer yes. We recognize so easily the importance of high self esteem in others. And we strive to build that positive self-image in our children, loved ones, friends and colleagues at work.

All the compliments and encouragement in the world offered to those we care about have very little effect compared to the example we show them. If you wish for your children to be positive people, secure in their self-esteem, you need only provide that role model for them by being a proud, happy, productive parent. Share joy and enthusiasm, confidence and perpetually positive self-talk.

Even if you have a negative spouse, negative friends, and a miserable environment, the process must begin with you, from within. You cannot work on those who surround you and put yourself off for later; it simply won't work that way.

Higher self esteem, in the form of positive mental images, is immediately available to you. Learn to focus on whatever is positive in your experience, and make this the basis for the beginning of your positive self-talk. Find identity with good things and positive people. We learn to like ourselves through practice. And in practicing high self esteem for ourselves, we provide others with a positive role model for their own growth.

**Human beings are
developed by mental
pictures.**

Twenty-Seven

An acorn grows into an oak tree. A tulip bulb develops into a tulip. For an acorn or a tulip, the energy and destiny are pre-set, genetically programmed and unavoidable.

A human being is completely different.

Yes, it is true that you will be male or female and you will have blue or brown eyes or male pattern baldness or a certain blood type or skin color because of genetics, but little of real importance in your life is genetically determined. Genetics does not determine whether the baby grows into a firefighter or a stockbroker, a university professor or a bank robber.

Human beings are developed by mental pictures.

Watch children to really get an insight into this process. The games of small children are almost entirely based on acting out mental pictures in the children's minds.

All those games of house, animal hospital, cops and robbers, prince and princess are grand experiments, and it is the work of childhood to try on many roles, selecting and discarding in a complex preparatory process.

If you have young children, observe closely and understand where their mental pictures are coming from. Do you like it that in your daughter's games she is always cast in the exclusively "mommy" role? What costume has your son chosen for Halloween this year? Children's mental images derive from what they are exposed to in books, television programs, and through real life models. Do you like what your children are learning? Who is teaching them?

As parents we should be so concerned about our role modeling. Have you ever noticed the child of a smoking parent walking around pretending to smoke? From 68% to 72% of children with smoking parents will also become smokers, while only 18—22% of those with nonsmoking parents will embrace this unhealthy habit.

You are very powerful in your child's life. Your words have a great impact on the mental images formed in your child's mind. What exactly are you describing most of the time?

In *What To Say When You Talk To Yourself* (Pocket Books, 1986), Shad Helmstetter, Ph.D. writes that "during the first eighteen years of our lives, if we grew up in fairly average, reasonably positive homes, we were told "No!," or what we could not do, more than 148,000 times!" In contrast, says Helmstetter, the number of times children are told what they can do or can accomplish probably amounts to no more than a few thousand.

When we're talking to our children, if we tell them all the bad that we see, they will grow up exactly the way we hoped they would NOT be. And remember, what we're doing as we raise our children is teaching them how to raise our grandchildren!

Growing up is a focusing process. We narrow our role choice and form habits of activity as we grow older, but we never lose the capacity to form and change our mental images.

BECOME CONSCIOUS OF YOUR MENTAL IMAGE OF YOURSELF. ARE YOU PLEASED WITH IT?

YOU are a package with a label on it...
how do you label yourself?

Twenty-Eight

You are a package with a label on it. Once you have a label attached, a whole course of events can ensue because of one little name.

Dr. Robert Rosenthal, an expert in what is known as expectations theory, conducted a now-famous experiment in the San Francisco Bay area schools.

At the beginning of the year, a school principal called three teachers into his office and informed them that because of their teaching excellence, they were to be assigned classes composed of the brightest children in the school. The children, he said, had been identified by IQ testing.

But, he added, so that they would not be accused of discriminating, the teachers were not to discuss this situation with the children or their parents or anyone. And the teachers were told to teach exactly as they were accustomed to teaching; they had, after all, been identified for their excellent methods. They were told to use the same curriculum, and that excellent results were expected.

And that's exactly what happened. The children did exceptionally well, and the teachers evaluated the experiment as very successful at the end of the year.

That's when they were told that it was all an elaborate fiction. The children had been selected arbitrarily. And so had the teachers. All of the exceptional results achieved were caused only by using labels—"excellent students" and "excellent teacher"— to create expectations of excellence— a classic self-fulfilling prophecy.

In education and in all other situations in life, we are quick to allow labels to predict outcomes. **But ultimately, the label attached to you is of your own creation.** When you meet someone for the first time, you are free, while still being completely honest, to label yourself in any way you choose, and describe the package contents as you see fit.

**The type of success that you
achieve is directly proportionate
to the mental pictures in your head.**

Twenty-Nine

Mental images are so important that we all have fairly clear pictures in our minds of ourselves engaged in the work we normally do. You can close your eyes and see yourself going about your work as a salesperson, a teacher, an astronaut, or whatever. You can get quite a vivid image of your office or whatever your work environment may be, and you can fill it in with real co-workers, clients, or customers. You can even move some imaginary people in and out of the picture.

Your picture will not stay static for long. A story will start to evolve, and those pictures will have an influence as you work towards an outcome.

Consider how you are permitting your stories to end. Do you tell success stories or stories of embarassment and failure? It really does make a difference. Just as you once imagined yourself into your present occupation, you continue to imagine the success you have in it. You are imagining success or failure all the time!

The type of success you are going to have in anything you do is in direct proportion to the mental pictures you have in your mind. Your mental pictures will determine your actions and your words, and they in turn will determine actual outcomes in your life.

How do you see yourself? Use your mental eye to recreate yourself—to blossom into the happy, productive person you want to be. It's up to you!

BECOME AWARE OF THE IMPORTANCE OF YOUR MENTAL PICTURES IN DETERMINING YOUR SUCCESS.

SAY IT!

SEE IT!!

SUPPORT IT!!!

SAY IT!
SEE IT!!
SUPPORT IT!!!

Thirty

Whenever you think of this book, I would like you to think of the three S's.

The first is SAY IT!

Say out loud the good things, the positive thoughts you have. Become super conscious of the self fulfilling prophesies that you create by what you say out loud and what you allow others to say to you.

The second is SEE IT!

Develop the ability to see your future—to see yourself achieving the goals that are important to you. See yourself as being a very proud, happy, productive person!

The third S is SUPPORT IT!

Support the mental image that you have of yourself to such an extent that it becomes a reality. Dress the part, act the part, become the part. Act it through until it is you!

The psychosomatic connection between your thoughts and your actions is absolute and complete when you express yourself in a positive way, when you carefully monitor the verbal input you allow into your mental computer, and when you hold positive, successful mental images. Then you will naturally follow through with the positive, constructive behavior that goes along with your beliefs, your values and your commitment.

With your mind in harmony with your activity, you will find new energy to pursue your goals, free of the old conflicts that inhibited the fulfillment of your dreams. You will be open to a new potential and possibilities that you will encounter in a remarkable, effortless way, when the process of personal transformation is set in motion in your life.

Now you understand the secret of the psychosomatic connection! Make it a living, breathing part of your daily life.

PART THREE

Recreate Yourself!

--High Achiever/Low Achiever—
The Choice is Yours!--

GREAT! NOW WE'RE GOING TO TALK ABOUT HOW YOU CAN MAKE THE CHANGES IN YOUR LIFE THAT ARE IMPORTANT TO YOU!

When I first got involved in my research about the 80/20 rule, I truly wanted to know if a person was born in the low achievement (or 80%) group or the high achievement (or 20%) group and stayed there, or if it was possible to move from one group into the other.

I selected eight people—four men and four women—to study. All were in the low achievement group—in fact, all were actually in the lower range of low achievers. Three had extremely low self images. All had come to me for counseling for various problems ranging from marital problems to weight control.

Since I wanted them to have an equity in the outcome of the experiment, I felt it was important that they also have a financial stake in it. So our agreement included a reduced fee for their therapy on my part and a promise on their part that they would follow my instructions and requests totally. I also expected a commitment of time from each of them—which included meeting with me for one hour each week.

The outcome was even greater than I had anticipated. Seven of the eight made fantastic progress and definitely moved from the low achievement group into the group of high achievers. (In fact, before the study was over I was actually envious of several of them!) Eight years later all seven continue to be high achievers and are certainly proof that it's very possible to move from one group to the other.

Although the eighth person (one of the men) did extremely well and is very pleased with the changes in his life, he was not quite able to move out of the 80% group. However, I'm still very proud of him and his mental and financial accomplishments.

How did we accomplish this fantastic transformation? Let me explain the procedure we used.

First, it's very important that you accept a basic concept about how the mind works. Dr. Shad Helmstetter gives this example which I believe explains it best.

Imagine examining the mind of a newly born infant—one just seconds old. What we would find would be a gigantic, infinite maze of hallways. Filling those hallways are millions and millions of filing cabinets—reaching from the floor to the ceiling on both sides and filling every inch of space.

If you were to open one of the drawers—any drawer—you would probably find it empty. For, except for a few basic natural instincts, such as the fear of falling or fear of the dark, the baby has not yet had any experiences or knowledge to store in his file drawers.

However, beginning immediately after birth and continuing as that child goes through life, every experience, everything he sees, hears, touches or feels—will be stored in one of those file drawers. And all that data will affect how he feels about himself, how he treats others, his likes and dislikes, prejudices, how he makes decisions, what makes him happy—even how much personal happiness there is in his life.

Now as this child travels through life, each time he comes to an intersection—a place where he must make a decision to turn one way or another—the choice he will make will be determined by the information stored in his filing cabinets. If he has more experiences and more knowledge on one side than the other, his file on that side will be more dominant and he will choose accordingly.

We see that all that was really keeping the people in our research group in the low achievement group were the limits placed on them by the information already stored in their file drawers. We now know that our lives are not programmed and set by the age of six or seven years. **We have the ability to make change in recreating ourselves thoughout our lifetime.**

Look at your own life and the changes you have made. You are not the same person you were five years ago, ten years ago—or even yesterday. **We have the ability to make changes and we change constantly.**

Possibly up to now a tremendous amount of the information stored in your file drawers has been placed there or influenced by others—with little or no control exercised by you.

For example, I live in Nebraska—BIG RED COUNTRY! And even though a few of us are not really football fans, every Saturday throughout the football season many of us wear our red sweaters and join in the Big Red mania as "our" team takes the field. When "our" team wins we feel great—and when it doesn't, we join the masses in speculating about what should have been done better or differently.

Why? Because in Nebraska during the football season everything from headlines to store displays, newscasts and general conversation is focused around the University of Nebraska football team. And the message which is repeated over and over in many different ways is simply this: if you live in Nebraska you've got to be a Big Red fan!

Now, I would guess that if those same non-fans moved to Denver, home of the Broncos, they'd probably be wearing orange and blue and cheering that team on to the Super Bowl—just like all the other Denverites!

Now, with your new awareness of the importance of what you say out loud and what you allow others to say out loud to you, you can take control of the information that goes into your mental computer. As with the research group, the data in your files may be all that's keeping you from being as happy, as productive, and as successful as you want to be and can be!

--Visualize Your Dreams of Success!--

What major process did our eight subjects use? **They simply learned how to create the success they desired by visualizing those successes as already having occurred, and then constantly reinforcing the image with positive affirmations.**

You see, your mind is not merely a memory bank where information and experiences are stored. I like to compare it to a diamond mine.

You know, a rough diamond is not easily identifiable to the untrained eye. In fact, it looks very much like a lump of coal. To have value it must be brought up out of the mine, and be cut and polished.

Your mind is the source of beautiful, valuable ideas. They are your own creations. But as with the rough diamonds, they must be brought forward into your consciousness through visualization and polished with affirmations.

Almost every university psychology class conducts this study, or a similar one, on the effectiveness of mental imagery.

Using three groups of ten people, each group goes to

a gym, and standing at the free throw line, each person takes a turn at shooting 100 baskets. Team and individual scores are kept.

For the next thirty days Team #1 will go to the gym daily and practice shooting baskets for one hour. Team #3 will also go to the gym daily, and in a totally relaxed position, with their eyes closed, will mentally practice successfully shooting baskets for one hour each day. Team #2 will neither visit the gym nor practice shooting baskets.

At the end of the thirty day period all three groups return to the gym for retesting. Team #1, who actually practiced shooting baskets, will improve their scores by 24 to 26%. Team #2, who did not even visit the gym during the thirty day period, will repeat scores almost identical to their original scores—with possibly a 1 to 2% improvement.

Team #3, who visualized themselves successfully shooting baskets, *will show an improvement rate of 22 to 25%*—almost as high as those who actually practiced. (And the best part is that they never missed a basket in their practice sessions!)

Through visualization you can replace negative self images and negative outcomes with highly positive images of total success. In other words, you see yourself as being exactly as you would like to be—and successfully doing the things you want to do!

The third basketball group didn't see themselves as being just better than they were in the test—they saw themselves throwing each ball expertly and successfully through the hoop. As Norman Vincent Peale writes in *The Positive Principle Today* (Fawcett Crest, 1977), "There is a deep tendency in human nature to become precisely what we image ourselves to be."

The members of the research group also used the power of visualization to turn into reality their dreams of success. They replaced their loser self image with ones of success and accomplishment!

--Music is the Connection!--

In a recent study reported by *USA TODAY*, " . . . mental imagery was shown to trigger an increase in specific disease-fighting cells, while leaving other cells unaffected." And adding music can boost the impact. According to Southern Methodist University music therapist Mark Rider and Dr. Jeanne Achterberg of the University of Texas Health Science Center in Dallas, " . . . 30 volunteers listened periodically to a 20 minute tape containing a relaxation message followed by music. They were asked to visualize specific types of blood cells being released in their bodies while listening to the tape. After six weeks, blood tests showed the only cell count that changed was the one they visualized, says Rider."

As you may have noticed, in this study music was used as a conduit for the mental imagery message in communication with the mind. Our resting heartbeat is approximately 60-70 beats per minute. Listening to music can either raise or lower our heartbeat, as well as other bodily activities.

But as we listen to music written in 4/4 time, or 60 beats per minute—particularly the largo movements of the Baroque concertoes—we find that two things begin to happen. First, our bodies begin to relax, and then our minds become very alert.

It's during that relaxed state of mind—known as *Alpha*—that our imaginations take over. Not only do we assimilate facts faster, but learning is actually accelerated and even more enjoyable! Super learning courses have long stressed the importance of using such music in making the mind more receptive to learning.

In our research group we used music as background

for the visualization process. By creating a state of relaxation our subjects were very open to the suggestions or affirmations that made up the third component of our experiment.

--Say It Again!--

Affirmations are nothing more than sentences or thoughts which provide the basis for the visualization process. Reminders of what we want to do or be or have. They must, of course, be very positive. And they must always be in the present tense—*I am, I have,* etc.. In our mind's eye we must see ourselves as already being successful as we create our new image.

The important thing to remember is that once our mind accepts a thought it becomes our own.

Beginning on page 178 you will find some examples of positive affirmations designed to help you get started in creating your own affirmations.

When I first started with the research group I used a method of deep relaxation during which I made positive verbal suggestions to the person. At the same time the person was creating the mental picture which had special significance for him or her.

It soon became apparent, however, that a weekly session of listening to positive suggestions was not nearly enough to override the years of negative data stored in their file drawers—no matter how relaxed they might become.

The advertising industry recognizes the value of repeating information over and over again. When a new commercial first appears on television, it is usually 60 seconds long. The name of the product is repeated several times, along with some catchy phrase or jingle that is designed to make an impact on your subconscious mind.

After appearing for a period of time the 60 second commercial is shortened to 45 seconds, then 30 seconds—and eventually it becomes just 10 seconds.

But even when you're listening to the 10 second version, your mind will automatically recall the message of the full 60 second commercial—if you've heard it often enough. Young children can often repeat verbatim the words to many commercials long before they know the alphabet or how to count.

Overriding the negative, limiting data in our file drawers requires constant repetition of the new positive thoughts. "We become what we think about most of the time," says Earl Nightengale.

So, we decided to adopt the same approach as the advertising industry. By creating audio cassette tapes which combined the 60 beats per minute music and positive affirmations, our eight people were able to listen to the suggestions several times each day—at their convenience. **By listening more frequently—and each time adding their own mental pictures of success—they were able to increase the volume of their new positive files much faster.**

Although the research group were encouraged to listen to the tapes several times each day, there were actually two times when listening had a greater effect on their minds. Early morning, just before getting up, and late evening, just before going to sleep, are times when we easily slip into the relaxed state of consciousness—*Alpha.*

By setting a timer to automatically turn on a cassette player about 10 minutes before the alarm wakened them, our subjects were able to reap the ultimate benefit of listening to their tapes of music and affirmations.

Listening to the tapes once again as they were drifting off to sleep gave their subconscious minds additional food for thought throughout the sleep process. And even though the words might not be heard by the conscious mind, once the mental picture had been brought into existence the subconscious mind was able to recall it completely.

Although I had previously used subliminal communication in my work, I was never truly pleased with the effectiveness or long term results. Now I believe the reason is that our minds function best and have greater retention when we think in pictures. If you have ever taken a memory improvement course, for example, you learned to associate mental pictures with what you wanted to remember.

However, since the message on a subliminal tape is heard only on the subconscious level, it is impossible to create a mental picture. (I also have a concern about the content of that subliminal message. I want to know and control the information which goes into my file drawers!)

There was one other requirement regarding the use of the tapes. It was imperative that the tapes be used daily for at least thirty days in succession. Slipping even one day had a negative effect, and it was necessary to begin all over again.

As the members of our group visualized themselves achieving their goals and dreams, their families and friends began to notice a change in them. And once they began to notice the changes themselves, the whole process seemed to accelerate. **And in time, they actually became the persons first created in their imaginations!**

VISUALIZATION + MUSIC + RELAXATION + AFFIRMATIONS = SUCCESS!

There you have it! The formula which helped our eight people change their lives from low achievement to high achievement and success!

Do you have a desire to be more successful, more productive, happier—to move from the 80%

group into the more elite 20% group of high achievement? If you're willing to invest your time and utilize your imagination YOU CAN become the person you want to be!

IF YOU CAN IMAGE IT,
YOU CAN POSSESS IT.

IF YOU CAN DREAM IT,
YOU CAN BECOME IT.

IF YOU CAN ENVISION IT,
YOU CAN ATTAIN IT.

IF YOU CAN PICTURE IT,
YOU CAN ACHIEVE IT.

—Author unknown

Beginning on this page are some examples of affirmations for a number of different situations. As you use them and others that you'll want to create for yourself, remember you must always form the mental picture of the words. **See yourself as already having successfully accomplished your goals.** Once you have formed the mental pictures your mind will accept the thought as your own. As you visualize the thought, repeat each statement *three times*—varying your tone and word emphasis slightly each time.

--WEIGHT CONTROL--

I take pride in my good eating habits.
I enjoy taking good care of my body.
I enjoy keeping my body's weight exactly
where I want it to be.
My desire for a slim, trim, healthy body is far stronger than
my desire for excess food.
I enjoy eating healthy foods that are good for me.

--HIGH SELF-ESTEEM--

I like who I am and I feel good about myself,
I have lots of energy and enthusiasm.
I enjoy working to improve myself each and every day.
I have many talents and skills and I enjoy developing and
using them.

--SMOKING--

I am proud that I do not smoke.
My desire for a healthy body is far stronger than
my desire to smoke.
Taking care of myself physically is very important to me.
I enjoy breathing clean air, being healthy, and being in
control of my mind and my body.
Every time I think about smoking my mind starts thinking
about all of the reasons why I do not smoke.

--SELF CONFIDENCE--

I am important!
People like me!
I see myself and my life in a positive way.
I enjoy finding positive and worthwhile qualities
in myself every day.
I really like myself!

--MEMORY--

I enjoy remembering names and faces, and I am
interested in the people I meet.
I remember conversations completely and clearly.
I enjoy listening completely and clearly.
I enjoy remembering anything that is important to me.

--DEVELOPING HIGH ENERGY--

I feel great!
My mind and my body work together like a beautiful team
pulling in the same direction.
I enjoy the extra energy that comes from within me.
My mind is sharp and clear!
I am physically fit and healthy.

--STRESS--

I am calm and confident.
I am living my life in a positive, worthwhile way.
I like who I am and I enjoy being me!
I enjoy focusing on my long range goals.
I am in control of my emotions.

--FREEDOM FROM WORRY--

I enjoy finding positive solutions.
I enjoy looking for constructive ways to make my life better.
I meet my responsibilities with enthusiasm and confidence
and enjoy the positive results.
Productive and positive thoughts come into my mind daily.

--SUCCESSFUL MARRIAGE--

I love my life and enjoy being married and sharing my life.
I enjoy the fact that my partner and I keep growing closer to
each other.
I keep discovering more and more ways to enjoy my
marriage and my family.
I enjoy having a partner to share information and
experiences with.

--TAKING RESPONSIBILITY--

I enjoy being accountable for my actions.
I am well organized, effective and efficient.
I assume full responsibility for my time and my actions.
This is a can do, will do, get things done day!

--CONTROLLING ANGER--

I am calm and thoughtful when faced with difficult
situations.
I enjoy being in control!
Each day I become more positive in my thoughts and
actions.
I enjoy outwardly expressing my love and concern for
others.

--CREATIVITY--

I have remarkable insights and expectations.
I enjoy my bursts of creative energy.
Creative thoughts and ideas come easily to me!
Life holds unlimited opportunities for me.

--TIME MANAGEMENT--

I enjoy doing the things I need to do and meeting deadlines.
I make good use of my time!
I enjoy deciding what is most important and giving it
priority.
Today is full of accomplishments and excellence.

--WINNING PERSONALITY--

People like to be around me.
I am warm and friendly.
My friendliness is genuine because I like, accept, and enjoy
other people.
I am trustworthy and responsible and people place a great
value on these qualities in me.

--SALES--

I am very successful at selling.
Creating new business comes naturally and easily for me.
I enjoy making good sales presentations and keeping myself
energetic and full of enthusiasm.
I enjoy the details of selling and give them my full attention.

--DECISION MAKING--

My choices are good and my judgement is sound.
My life is better every day because I make good decisions
quickly.
I trust my judgement and have faith in myself and my
abilities.
I look forward to the positive, successful outcomes of any
decision that I make.

--CREATING HOPE--

I am strong and I have the strength I need to see me through
the situations that are important to me.
I expect solutions. I look for them and they always come.
I have faith. I have courage. And I have belief in myself.
I am a winner, and I give myself the energy and the belief to
come up with positive solutions.

--FINANCIAL FREEDOM--

I enjoy the financial independence that I achieve and the
freedom that comes with it.
I visualize my financial goals in my mind every day and I see
myself achieving and deserving the goals that I set.
I am successful and I'm on my way to even greater financial
achievement and independence.
I am financially responsible and I lead my life that way.

--VISUALIZATION--

I have learned to picture my own success in advance
in my mind.
I enjoy visualizing future events and seeing them clearly.
I accept the resonsibility for my own thoughts and enjoy
having those thoughts and mental pictures creating my future
in the most positive way.
I visualize myself as successful, healthy, happy and having
great peace of mind.

--LIVING TODAY--

My energy is high and I enjoy taking care of
myself every day.
I learn something new every day.
Today is a great day for me!
My future looks bright and I enjoy planning and preparing
for it.

YES, YOU CAN begin now to make the changes in your life that are important to you. To help you get started, Raymond has created a series of cassette tapes. They cover a wide range of topics including:

———— WEIGHT CONTROL/ DECISION MAKING
———— SMOKING/ DEVELOPING HIGH ENERGY
———— SUCCESSFUL MARRIAGE/ LIVING TODAY
———— STRESS/ FREEDOM FROM WORRY
———— SALES/ FINANCIAL FREEDOM
———— MEMORY/ CREATIVITY
———— CONTROLLING ANGER/ WINNING PERSONALITY
———— TIME MANAGEMENT/ TAKING RESPONSIBILITY
———— HIGH SELF ESTEEM/ SELF CONFIDENCE
———— VISUALIZATION/ CREATING HOPE

You may order ANY three tapes for $29.95, ANY six tapes for $39.95, or all ten tapes for $49.95. Prices include postage and handling.

PLEASE SEND THE TAPES I'VE SELECTED ABOVE TO:

Name: _____

Address: _____

City, State _____

Zip Code _____

I've enclosed my check for $ _____

Please charge to my VISA/MASTER CHARGE card account.
My number is _____
Expiration date_____

Send your order to:
Raymond Lemke
8031 West Center Road, Suite 222
Omaha, Nebraska 68124
Or call 1-800-356-2233

WOULD YOU LIKE TO ORDER ADDITIONAL
COPIES OF:

YES, YOU CAN!

YES! Please send me_____ copies of *Yes, You Can!* I've enclosed my check for $7.95 per copy. (Postage and handling included.)

YES! Please charge_____copies of *Yes, You Can!* to my VISA/ MASTER CHARGE account.

My number is ————————————————————

Expiration date ————————————————————

Send my books to:

Name ——————————————————————————

Address ——————————————————————————

City, State ——————————————————————————

Zip Code ——————————————————————————

Sent to:

Raymond Lemke
8031 West Center Road, Suite 222
Omaha, Nebraska 68124

Or phone: 1-800-356-2233

For information regarding special prices for groups, please contact Mr. Lemke at the above address.

RAYMOND LEMKE

A DYNAMIC, ENERGETIC
SPEAKER

Raymond Lemke is considered by many to be a leading spokesman in the field of Human Resource Development. He has an uncanny ability to translate complex psychological theories into practical, useful techniques that people in every walk of life can understand and utilize immediately.

His timely topics cover 5 important areas:

1. Sales

2. Management

3. Personal Happiness and Productivity

4. Customer Service

5. Spouse Program

If you'd like to have Raymond speak at your next meeting or convention, please write or call :

8031 W. Center Rd., Suite 222
Omaha, NE 68124
or call 1-402-391-5540
or 1-800-356-2233

MAUN - LEMKE

Maun - Lemke is a national speaking, consulting, and research firm. Our business efforts are focused on numerous types of health care and human service organizations. Our firm, founded in 1984, is dedicated to assisting health care and human service organizations in meeting the challenges of providing correct services and products to their customers.

When Clint Maun and Raymond Lemke founded the company, they started with 3 basic principles which are still utilized to this day. They are:

1. Speakers, consultants, and researchers can only help with 3 important areas - *Revenue Enhancement, Cost Containment,* and *Quality Improvement.* We focus our work with clients in an area, as identified by the client, with specific end objectives designed.

2. Our work is "boil-down" in nature. We provide solutions, skills, tips, techniques, and ideas as facilitators, speakers, researchers, catalysts, and consultants. We never "boil-up" or evoke more problems.

3. We offer a 100%, Unconditional, Money Back Guarantee on All of our work!

Our firm's work currently includes active efforts in diverse business divisions.

Maun - Lemke is one of the nationally recognized leaders in speaking, consulting, and research!